MUNITION LASSES

MISS LILIAN BARKER, C.B.E.,
Lady Superintendent.

MUNITION LASSES

Six Months as Principal Overlooker in Danger Buildings

BY

A. K. FOXWELL

M.A., D.LITT.

The Naval & Military Press Ltd

Published by

The Naval & Military Press Ltd
Unit 5 Riverside, Brambleside
Bellbrook Industrial Estate
Uckfield, East Sussex
TN22 1QQ England

Tel: +44 (0)1825 749494

www.naval-military-press.com
www.nmarchive.com

*In reprinting in facsimile from the original, any imperfections are inevitably reproduced
and the quality may fall short of modern type and cartographic standards.*

DEDICATION TO
THE CAP AND DETONATOR GIRLS

My Dear Lasses,

I dedicate this little book to you in affectionate remembrance of our work in Woolwich Arsenal in the Third Year of the War, from July 1916 to January 1917.

In the beginning of last year, as most of you know, a few women were admitted into the Arsenal to work on munitions. As the weeks wore on, these women proved themselves capable and worthy of the trust reposed in them, and earned the praise and confidence of those in authority by their quickness at learning, their deftness in the operations, their pluck and eagerness in all their undertakings.

The six months' work amongst you as Principal Overlooker, under conditions hitherto foreign to our experience and comprehension, has added a richness to life, fraught with a deeper, sincerer knowledge of humanity—a knowledge attained equally through the pleasures and many-sided interests, as through the anxieties and difficulties incidental to such work in the Danger Buildings of the Arsenal.

And when, at the beginning of the year, I had

permission from my chief to visit the other factories where women were employed, I encountered familiar faces wherever I went. Not only old friends presiding over examiners' tables, and college chums acting as overlookers in the "streets" of vast machinery shops, but whatever factory I visited, in one workshop or other, a flutter of excitement animated the workers, and an eager whisper of "It's *our* P.O.," caused me to scan the faces more closely, thereby discovering one of my old Cap and Detonator Girls. I found you, lasses, in Primer and in Fuse, in Cordite and in Trotyl, in the Cartridge, and in the Fuse and Case Factories. I feel, therefore, that I can address you all, wherever you are in Woolwich Arsenal, as a memento of our work together in the Arsenal.

So that in years to come, when you have your grandchildren at your knees, you may tell them how you supplied your fathers and husbands, your brothers and sweethearts, with munitions by land and by sea ; and by so doing helped to keep the torch of Britain alight, and the flag of her Empire flying free, in the years of the Great War 1914—

I am always,

Your sincere well-wisher and
Principal Overlooker,

A. K. FOXWELL.

HARROW-ON-THE-HILL,
September 1917.

ABBREVIATIONS IN TEXT

L.S.   = Lady Superintendent.
P.O.   = Principal Overlooker.
D.P.O. = Principal Overlooker of Danger Buildings.
M.O.   = Medical Officer.

PREFATORY NOTE

THIS little volume is intended to give the general public an insight into the life of the Munition Worker—a life which, while sympathetically spoken of by the nation at large, and at last included in the nation's prayers, is practically unknown to all but the initiated.

The reader will readily understand why the work is not discussed in detail. Indeed, though every care was taken to refrain from mentioning what might be against the Empire's interest to divulge, stars in several places denote the use of the Censor's pencil. A time may come, at the end of the war, when I may be permitted to speak more fully of the technical side of the woman's work in munitions. Meanwhile I am very grateful to the authorities for permission to publish some account of life in the Arsenal, whose sacred precincts have hitherto escaped the invasion of the daring chronicler.

My thanks are due to Messrs Macmillan, and Sidgwick & Jackson, for permission to quote from the poems of Sir Rabindranath Tagore and Rupert Brooke respectively; to the Panora, Tasma, and Fancy Dress Studios for permission to use their photographs in illustrations; and to all those in authority, both men and women, who have given me facilities for seeing factories, canteens, and hostels.

A. K. F.

CONTENTS

7

MUNITION LASSES

CHAPTER I

GETTING IN

"They have their exits and their entrances."
SHAKSPEARE.

ONE memorable day last year, the Registrar
for the University Women's War Service
invited me to go to Woolwich, there to be
interviewed as a candidate for the supervision
of the women workers in the Danger Buildings of the Arsenal.

Finding that many ways led to the destination, Beresford Square, Woolwich, by train,
motor-bus, or tram, the train route was chosen
for the sake of speed ; though experience, then
and subsequently, taught that no route whatever could lay any claims to celerity.

The journey lacked tediousness owing to
the interest of travelling part of the way with
a Canadian, who was overflowing with patriotism, and pride in England's greatness.   As we

steamed out of Charing Cross Station and over the river there came into view that majestic scene which Wordsworth has described so feelingly: [1]

> " Earth hath not anything to show more fair ;
> Dull would he be of soul who could pass by
> A sight so touching in its majesty :
> This city now doth like a garment wear
> The beauty of the morning ; silent, bare,
> Ships, towers, domes, theatres, and temples lie. . . "

The Canadian scanned river and Houses of Parliament, the stately pile of the Abbey, and St Stephen's Tower, and as his eye caught sight of the Union Jack floating over Big Ben, he broke forth eagerly : " Ah, that little rag ! that there little bit of rag ; 'twill take every Jack of our Navy, and every lad of us to pull it down. That little rag floatin' there so free tells us what we're in for."

These words brought home to me once again what women "were in for " : making munitions to keep our sailors and soldiers bravely fighting on until the day of victory shall be ours ; to keep that flag floating over our Empire's Citadel, and to hoist again the flags of our brave Allies.

Woolwich, as everyone knows, has its Dock-

---

[1] "On Westminster Bridge "—Sonnet.

yard, its Arsenal, and its Military College. Since the war, however, Woolwich and the Arsenal are interchangeable terms. Seen from Woolwich Common, it has a certain dignity; approached by way of Powis Street the main gates are sufficiently impressive; but nothing on this earth could prepare us for Beresford Square, except Beresford Square itself, and it bursts upon our vision with greater intensity if we approach it from Woolwich Arsenal railway station, cross the road and turn left into the kind of " Petticoat Lane " entry of the Square.

We are then in pandemonium, and before us are the main gates of the Arsenal. Into the Square at this point from four main thoroughfares pours an endless stream of traffic —omnibus, tram, and motor-lorry; but no taxi, no private motor to be seen, only an occasional Arsenal car driven by a khaki-clad woman wearing on her shoulder straps the letters O.F.

Except for a passage kept sufficiently clear for vehicles approaching the terminus, the Square presents at all hours a dense mass of humanity. Alongside and on the main pavement, as well as on all sides of the Square,

are ranged on the roadway the covered booths, where everything may be bought in the way of clothing, household utensils, and food, provided that one's ambitions are not too lofty in the matter of household needs, nor one's ideas too delicate in the manner of dress.

The booths are constant and ubiquitous, yet they increase at the end of the week, supplying a greater variety of food and live stock, when not only chickens and ducks, but pets in the shape of dogs and birds are on sale; even parrots, and an occasional dignified cockatoo with yellow crest may be seen; but one feels that these birds are singularly out of place, and would willingly see them transferred to the Zoo, or to some destination providing a better school for learning the English language in a less lurid, more polite form.[1]

Every Saturday, and on Sunday morning, the upper side of the Square presents a glow of colour from the huge flower-booths set up: booths suggesting so marked a resemblance to the street corner flower-markets seen abroad that one concludes that a Belgian

[1] Owing, doubtless, to Food Economy the live stock is now strictly utilitarian.

or French market-gardener is plying her trade
here, and earning a livelihood for the period
of the war by selling flowers and plants to
the Arsenal munition workers.

These flowers and an adjacent fruit-stall
with its well-arranged piles of fruit relieve
the scene from sordidness; and so what first
repels, attracts, and the elements of flowers
and fruit are an earnest of what we shall
discover in the life of the Arsenal. Many
a story could be told of the ultimate experience of the flower-stalls: how one worker,
tired and fagged herself, buys a few flowers
to cheer an invalid mother, and in the buying
forgets her own fatigue; how another carries
back to her hostel a handful of Michaelmas
daisies to cheer a sick mate; how another
still, goes off proudly with a many-coloured
posy for her sweatheart, who is lying wounded
in the Herbert Hospital; and sometimes
with footsteps sad and slow, and merriment
dimmed for a time, a group of workers chooses
a wreath or a cross for some comrade who
has died.

We must not linger too long in Beresford
Square, for candidates provided with green
tickets of admission from the Labour Ex-

change opposite the station, or with letters of introduction from the Ministry of Munitions, must proceed to the gate, a matter of a half-penny tram fare from Beresford Square. This journey takes any time between three and twenty-three minutes, according to the exigencies of the traffic. The sight of ten or twelve L.C.C. trams, motionless at either side of a short single line, waiting for trams to pass up and down alternately, is not uncommon when the number of passengers is excessive at the beginning and end of shifts.

The fates are auspicious on this occasion, and the entrance gate is soon reached. Here facetious tram conductors call out: "This way to Plumstead and bedstead" to the weary but chattering workers, who stream up the steps from the gate morning and evening.

To gain entrance to the Arsenal, the new-comer must cautiously descend the wide flight of steps partitioned off by iron rails into sections. This rail is a necessity during the ebb and flow of humanity at the beginning and end of each shift.

Entering the gates beyond, severely scrutinised by sentry and police, who examine our admission passes, we turn to a shed-like building somewhat similar to a waiting room at a wayside station. This is the office of the Lady Superintendent, under whose organising genius and powerful personality the arrangements relating to the women in the Arsenal are carried out.

A well-balanced temperament justly poised between power and kindliness, strenuous effort and womanly sympathy, she sets up a standard of straightness and fairness which touches all classes and reaches out to the farthest corners of the Arsenal; and she expects and obtains from everybody around her the highest effort and the best work. With a strong brain, a firm hand, a kindly smile, and imperturbable countenance amidst the greatest pressure of work, she stands "four square to every breeze that blows"—and, to follow up the metaphor, it is not only a fair breeze, but at times a strong sou'-wester—in dealing with the vast organisation. This includes, beyond interviewing and placing candidates, their health, discipline, and housing, the social side, with recreation clubs and classes, medical officers' reports, and Welfare Workers. But the breeze always subsides, for to every difficulty she

2

applies a fund of humour which brings her triumphantly through.

The L.S. Office consists of a good-sized room where candidates are interviewed, with a small type-writer's office opening out of the larger room. This small office communicates with the private room of the L.S. Furnished with Spartan-like simplicity, it contains desk, chair, a side-table, and a few photographic groups of the workers on the walls.

The scene in the Interviewing Room is one of orderly disorder. A central table faces a bench running alongside the wall close to the door, where the candidates sit in batches of sixteen. An outer shed shelters the surplus number.

Like the fabled Mercury of the underworld, a doorkeeper marshals the forces, keeping back the crowd and gathering in those fortunate ones whose turn it is to be admitted. With the skill due to long practice he keeps the interviewing bench supplied with sixteen applicants, succeeding by alternate harshness and kindliness in squeezing the correct numerical total into the available space. All goes well provided the bench is filled with sixteen average-sized women; but, as in omnibus or train, one or two overweights cause a bulging in the line, and various countenances wear anxious or chastened expressions as they are partially submerged by one or two of the more buxom type.

Above the candidates are shelves containing stationery. Over the stove on the door side are more shelves filled with correspondence files. Behind the central table a series of small tables are occupied by clerks and Welfare Workers engaged in writing reports, making out discharges, or filing the blue entry papers. The L.S. or her deputy sits at the central table and interviews the candidates in pairs.

Questioning proceeds somewhat as follows:

" What age are you?" " Twenty-three, miss." " And you?" " Twenty-one." " I have no vacancies except for Danger Buildings. Are you willing to enter and work in mercury?" " Yes, miss." " Well, take this blue paper, and you will be shown outside how to fill it in."

Then the next two are called.

" How old are you?" " Twenty-eight." " And you?" " Nineteen." (To the elder) " Are you willing to work in yellow powder?"

" What's that ? "   " Trotyl."   " Well, miss,
I have my husband at the front, and my
children to look after; I don't feel I ought
to run the risk."   " There are other things
to do; you look strong; you might undertake
trucking."   " Yes, miss, and may my friend
work with me ? "   " No, I can't put your friend
there with you, but she can go to the next
factory, and you will be able to take your meals
together in the same canteen."   They go away
content, with the blue paper to be filled in.

The monotony of interviewing new candidates is relieved by occasional demands from
some worker or other.

A woman who has been six hours in the
Danger Buildings says she cannot possibly
stand it.   She is all of a tremble.   No reassur-
ing statement that her fear is groundless dis-
arms her.   One feels that she is better elsewhere, doing work requiring no nerve strain.
Such an incident as this is extraordinarily
uncommon.   The majority of our women enter
and take to their unaccustomed tasks as to
the manner born.

Another woman insists upon seeing the
L.S.   She has been in the Arsenal one day,
and objects to wearing the regulation cap.

" The wearing of a cap is one of the regulations," says the L.S. " This is where woman's work comes in — not only doing the work required, but willingly submitting to discipline. We are His Majesty's servants, and, like the men at the front, we must be obedient to regulations." The woman goes away silenced.

As a rule a kindly word or a smile restores confidence. A remark such as, " You will help our soldiers in the trenches by filling the shells and getting the war over," sends another candidate away proud in the thought that she also is able to take her part in the nation's need ; and this aspect of the case is new and delightful to some workers, setting up an ideal that lifts her above the sordidness of what has been hitherto daily toil for the mere necessity of bread to be earned.

The next candidate is one of the Sarah Gamp type, with the central part of her physiognomy flushed and a suspicious watering of the eye. " How old are you ? " inquires the figure at the central table. A plaintive look is followed by an indignant expression at being questioned on so delicate a subject, but no reply is forthcoming. At a third repetition, " How *old* are you? "

the grudging answer comes: " Er, forty-five."
" What were you doing before you came here ?"
" Doin' ! I ain't bein' doin' nothin' ; leastways
for eight years . . ." Her voice resumes in
more determined tones : " I bin doin' a bit
of washin' to keep myself together." Her
features settle into a fierce hostility, as if
daring contradiction. She receives a yellow
slip of paper and is told to come next week
to see if there is anything for her.

A Welfare Worker will probably investigate
her case. Such women, if they have merely
been unfortunate, may be set to do some good
work in scrubbing, and may settle down quite
successfully under a firm and kind hand.
They regain their self-respect in the knowledge of work honestly done with other workers
for some good end.

And so the candidates stream along, and
before the day is ended hundreds may have
passed through and gone on to be medically
examined. All classes and conditions enter :
the young, the elderly, the keen, the sad-eyed,
peer's daughter and daughter of toil, university
graduate and professional woman, all ready to
lift their burden in whatever form it may be
required.

And all this work revolves round the L.S., whose splendid physique and cheery forcefulness dominates the whole staff. In the midst of marshalling the candidates by the doorkeeper, the interviewing by the secretary at the central table, the conversation of the Welfare Workers over their inspection work, and the monotone of one poor Welfare Visitor who has to visit an absentee at her home in Stratford, and, not knowing how to get there, relieves her mind by murmuring at intervals, "Oxford St., Stratford, E.," as she turns over the pages of an A.B.C. and studies a map of London: above all these minor sounds is heard the firm tones of our L.S.: "Now, look at one another, you two." The remark is addressed to two strangers just appointed by her to the same factory. A general laugh ensues, and she adds: "It's good to meet a face that you can pick out in a crowd, you know; you'll be glad to recognise one another in the factory to-morrow."

Sometimes, to the enjoyment of her staff, our L.S. takes the central table. The candidates pass briskly through her hands, though not without interruptions, such as telephone replies, urgent questions from a Welfare Visitor, or an immediate slight readjustment of canteen administration. Every candidate gives her age and previous calling, and is appointed to work suitable to her age and strength.

Occasionally, a timid question as to the particular dangers of Danger Buildings elicits the remark: "You girls seem to think that we have a little cemetery tucked away in a corner of the Arsenal, where *hundreds* of people are buried who have been blown up. We don't have these excitements here. Sometimes a girl burns her fingers when she puts them in the wrong place, but you can do that quite as easily at home." Then the cheery voice continues: "However, this is war work, so we don't expect to get a leisurely job. Aren't you willing to do your bit, like the soldiers in the trenches? We mustn't expect *our* work to be easy."

The candidate, seeing the matter more clearly, assents; and the next two, having listened to the previous conversation, state their willingness to go into Danger Buildings.

"That's the right spirit," comments the L.S. "That sort of thing is going to end the war." They are thus rapidly interviewed with a manner and tone that fits each candidate.

Those who are interviewed as Principal Overlookers are sent on after a talk with the L.S. to the manager of the group of factories to which they are assigned. I shall not soon forget the courteous manner of Mr X—— as he chatted about the duties of Principal Overlookers in Danger Buildings. And as he set forth his views of work and the need for an optimistic standpoint, one felt in him a kindred spirit. "While holding an ideal in view," he said, "it is necessary to keep in reserve a sympathetic tact for the actual achievement, and never be unduly cast down at the difference between ideal and achievement." Many a time his words proved helpful on difficult days, when hands were short, machines troublesome, or gowns scarce.

The rule was adopted at the outset of dropping every difficulty at the end of the day, and starting the morrow perfectly clear, never going back to what was past, unless necessary. In this way a reserve of energy was husbanded.

The business of entering His Majesty's Service in the Arsenal is not complete until we have passed the doctors and been registered. Registration takes time. At length a registered number and rule book is handed to us with instructions to present ourselves at a certain hour and place in the Arsenal the following Monday morning.

The rule book is inscribed with the factory to which we are assigned, and our rank in that factory. We are now definitely His Majesty's servants in Woolwich Arsenal, and under penalties not to take work elsewhere until we shall be properly discharged, and have received our clearance paper.

For better or for worse we have joined the Munition Army, and before us is the " Great Unknown."

CHAPTER II

THE MUNITION ARMY

" But to this 'sembly runnyng in the waye
My strength fayleth to reche it at the full."
Sir Thomas Wiat.

THE streams of humanity that flow in and out
through the many gates of the Arsenal arouse
a feeling of amazement, amounting to awe.
The gate through which the newcomer enters
might be termed the Labour Gate, for the
majority have their entrance there. Standing
on slightly rising ground, it affords to the
observer an extended and comprehensive view
of the outgoing shift as of a mighty river.
It gathers impetus as it nears the gate, fed by
the many tributaries and streams of workers
who enter the main road by more devious ways
towards the end of the journey to the Arsenal
gates, and thence home. The outgoing stream
is perhaps more turbulent, more swift of movement, more oblivious to any obstacles in its

path than the incoming one; for there are
trains to catch and trams to mount in the least
possible time in order to secure a few minutes'
more rest before the inevitable summons back
to labour. It requires a considerable amount
of force, or insistent pleasantry, on the part of
the women workers to gain a seat on these
occasions; acrobatic accomplishments are also
a distinct advantage to the attainment of this
end. For those who cannot mount by the
ordinary method are not seldom seen to climb
the rail, or swarm over the steering gear, and
mount to the upper part of the tram by means
of the balustrade instead of by the stairway
itself, so eager are the crowds to return home
by the first available means of transit to their
breakfast, dinner, and bed.

For these reasons we were continually grateful that supervision duties called us earlier and
kept us later, so that we were scarcely ever
drawn into this human whirlpool with its very
remote chance of obtaining a seat.

The incoming stream varies in its movement,
according to the time. The early comers
enter at a leisurely pace, but as the hour nears
6.30 and the bell clangs out, the pace increases,
and those who are late in starting or who

have been detained by congestion of traffic and are anxious to pick up their ticket in time, make frantic and ineffectual attempts to break through the main human stream, and hurry to their destination. The ticket denotes the punctual attendance and the presence in the factory of each worker. Those who fail to pick up their ticket are returned as late on the time-sheets. This rule is adhered to even if lateness is enforced by such reasons as breakdown of traffic, since it is impossible to find out with such vast numbers the reasons for lateness. To misquote a well-known phrase, the Arsenal may be divided into three classes of degrees of lateness, where " Some are born *late*, others achieve *lateness*, others have *lateness* thrust upon them."[1] No one escapes lateness in wintry weather, when trains are behind time and trams break down, while fog dislocates traffic altogether; others again, prone to punctuality, through unwonted length of hours of labour and shortening of their normal time of sleep are at times unable to rise through sheer exhaustion, at the appointed moment.

The great anxiety of the newcomer is to

[1] " Some men are born great . . . them."—SHAKSPEARE.

arrive in time, and it is a marked day in one's experience to rise for the first time at 5 a.m., breakfast, and set off to work while the whole world seems given over to repose. We find ourselves at 6.20 on a summer's morning gazing at the immense crowd. Being quite ignorant of the next step, we consult a policeman and are told that new entries wait for the guide. So we watch the mighty stream of humanity with bewilderment, if not indeed trepidation. The great bell at the gateway clangs out the final summons. It is a friendly five minutes' call to those who work in the great machinery factories near by, but its raucous tones spell lateness to the workers whose business lies far away in Danger Buildings. The surging tide slackens, becomes an eddy, and an official appears, saying, "Come along, you new entries, I will show you where to go. Now then, women on one side, men on the other." So we are divided, as it were, into sheep and goats, and we are herded up a long road.

Railway lines run alongside, and cross and recross our path at frequent intervals ; engines scream along to our right, our left, in front. Huge war-lorries bear down upon us and scatter us. We think of Lady Macbeth's injunction: " Screw your courage to the stick-ing-place," and derive comfort from the con-vincing conclusion of her spirited " and we'll not fail." So we brace ourselves somewhat as follows: " Remember this is war work: no indulgence in the matter of paved ways or footpaths for pedestrians: leave out of calcula-tion all that is not absolutely necessary; we are merely parts of a vast war machine that must go as smoothly and as swiftly as possible until such time as honourable Peace crowns the nation's efforts. This walk is the outward symbol of the stern meaning of war."

At the entrance to the Danger Buildings the men undergo a rigorous search of pockets for matches and tobacco. The women are asked, as in crossing the frontier in those far-off days of peace, " to declare," and we are on the point of saying soothingly (as of yore to those Eumenides of the Customs, who had it in their power to render us abjectly comfort-less, if such was their will), " Non, monsieur, rien du tout, rien à déclarer." The feeling of levity is hastily subdued, and we proceed onward to the women's Shifting-house a few yards further away in the factory to which we have been appointed.

This journey was a mild harbinger of the twice daily, or nightly, route to be taken. In hot August days the heat was stifling and the dust suffocating; in the wet days of October, and the rampantly torrential nights of November, we waded ankle deep in mud and water, arriving with shoes, stockings, and goloshes soaked. Again, in parts of December our footsteps rang like iron on the frost-bound mud, and our senses tingled and our spirits rose under the exhilaration of the keen frosty air. Then the blackness! But this was no peculiar attribute to Arsenal life, as everybody knows. The very occasional lamps dazzled the eye with the unaccustomed gleam, making us still more blind. The last part of the way was a plunge through a miniature lake of mud to the Ticket Office, evidently built by some brilliant architect a few inches above the surrounding level to prevent its complete inundation. But here as elsewhere, and always, the authorities did their best to lessen discomfort for their women workers. Holes were filled in and damaged roads mended as quickly as it was possible; but a more level roadway could never do away with the Arsenal mud, which is historic.

" Here we are," a gruff voice might be heard saying in the darkness, possibly proceeding from a man of thirty years' standing in the Arsenal: " Here we are, same old Arsenal mud, same old mud-holes."

So you will see the way of duty had its difficulties, as we have been taught; but, unlike the Scriptural context, it was very prone to lead to disaster. Those, however, who have trodden this way, grappling with their work to the best of their ability, have felt the joy that comes from struggling, in the thought that because of these rough places they can claim a part in real war work: that is, war work shorn of comfort, luxury, or indulgence. Such work wants no praise; it carries its own joy—the joy of difficult work accomplished.

> " He that walks it . . .
> He shall find the stubborn thistle bursting
> Into glossy purple." [1]

Those of us who have walked there and look back in reminiscence, remember no more the thistles, but see, all along the track, the purple patches.

Other ways lead to the Danger Buildings: the wide road with the pedestrians' platformed

[1] "Ode to Wellington."—TENNYSON.

side-walk, with a pleasant view of low-lying
country interspersed with streams, and a variety
of marshland vegetation. The third way has
some claims to natural effects, and might be
called the Historic Way. We enter through
the massive main gates fronting Beresford
Square, and, leaving the residential court, we
pass the inspiring statue of youthful Wellington, which suggests virile strength in every
line of the figure, forceful purpose in the
poise of the head, noble resolve in every
feature of the keen face.

The Historic Way affords a glimpse of river
bank whose distant edge is fringed with low
scrub, allowing all the wealth of colour of a
fine sunset to be reflected in its waters —
water that takes on an opaline hue when the
masses of golden cloud settle down into broad
lines of crimson and purple; when steamboat
and tug, small river craft and coal-barge appear
like " painted ships upon a painted ocean," in
that still period of evening when day, panopled
with subdued splendour of colour, goes forth beyond the sunset; and night, wrapped about with
dewy veil and star-wrought garment, comes to
brood over all, as Nature sinks into repose.

Many a Sunday evening in summer and

autumn we have felt the calm beauty of this way, and sung an evensong with the rest of Nature, enjoying the quietude before the noise of many footsteps and the hum of voices called once more to work. Another glance at the river, then over the footbridge and away to our factory. Though we lose sight of the river, it runs parallel to us, and occasionally we catch a pleasant glimpse of the tawny sails of the river craft floating against a background of sky like some graceful bird. Thus our factory is richly endowed in its surroundings. That tawny sail floating past is on its way to Greenwich; in the other direction lies Gravesend. What a wealth of historic association lies in and between these two ports! But four centuries ago, King Harry at Greenwich was dividing his time between hunting in the Abbey woods and planning out his schemes with keen diplomatic genius for the greatness of England, the placing her side by side with her powerful continental neighbours. And we remember how his ambassador landed at Gravesend, and posted up to Greenwich, breathless with news from the Imperial Charles, to meet the King. And on the way, he, Sir Thomas Wiat,

courtier, ambassador, poet, wrote the patriotic
lines in his exultation at reaching England
once more. ' Tagus, farewell," he exclaims ;
'"for I go to meet the Thames, to seek my
King and country, alone for whom I live."
King Harry and Wiat began, what Elizabeth
in her palace at Greenwich saw consummated
fifty years later. Greenwich to-day wears the
ineffaceable marks of its pageant, and power,
and bravery, in the days of the defeat of the
great Armada : such days repeated under
Nelson, when its old glories were revived and
an added lustre given. And to-day our sailor
lads of the training school march proudly
through its streets, knowing that Greenwich
is one of the precious stones of our Empire,
ringing as it does with Britain's mastery of
the seas.

So along Straightway, and Broadway, and
Riverway the women munition workers pass
to their labour. Here and there on the way
lies some vast workshop where man-power is
still required for forge or for gunnery. That
forge, for example, with its huge furnaces
and ringing sounds of hammering steel, whose
interior vividly contrasts with the outer darkness, might have given Turner a subject

symbolic of Light, Force, and Darkness, as
companion to his " Rain, Steam, and Speed ";
or provided Dante with another passage for his
Purgatorio.

Two traits are noticeable in the munition
worker as she journeys to and from her factory
—an unquenchable flow of spirits, and a liking
for gay attire. Silk stockings and velvet shoes
happily gave way in the autumn weather to
more serviceable boots and gaiters. Great
attention is paid to the head-dress and the
arrangement of the hair; and this is a re-
markable and delightful fact, because every
hairpin must be discarded on reaching the
Shifting-house, and there is no space for any
elaboration of toilet. It does the lasses credit
that everyone turns out fresh and neat, even
gay, at the close of the shift, in spite of
having no convenience and no aid for personal
decoration.

Every woman carries either an attaché case,
or a light bag made of straw containing
provisions, and crockery for making tea, including a special teapot.

The conversation up the Straight reminds
one of a game played as children with slips of
paper and questions to be answered, every slip

of paper changing hands after each answer. The conversation, like the game, generally revolved round the questions: what his name was; what hers; when they met; what he said, and what she said; and the result of it all. The reality, like the game, is provocative of much laughter.

Sometimes we heard hurrying footsteps behind, and one of my girls cried out, "Good evening, miss; you're always early, aren't you?" and she would proceed to chat of her work in the factory and her home life. Our girls had a wonderful facility at conversation, talking to and from their work, and at their work, and never at a loss for a word. Sometimes a young mother would chat about her little son, the image of his father in France; another would talk of her sailor brother, and of her efforts to mother younger brothers and sisters. So these talks helped us to learn to know one another, and relieved the monotony of the walk to the Shifting-house and the twelve hours' work that lay before us.

CHAPTER III

" Oh, the little more and how much it is,
And the little less and what worlds away ! "
BROWNING.

THE Shifting-house of all Danger Buildings
is the threshold of the factory. By Shifting-
house alone are all employees admitted, and
thence pass out to their respective workshops,
when they have been searched and are suitably clad.

The great machinery shops of non-danger
buildings engaged in such work as shell-case.
fuse, cartridge, and T-tube cases have their
respective cloakrooms adjoining the shops.
In one large factory near the gates, the cloak-
room opens out of the vast workshop, and
entry is first made by the workshop door.
There are also rows of pegs placed down the
entire length of the building, where the out-
door garments hang.

37

In the Tailor's Shop, that teeming hive of sempstresses, machinists, and tailoresses, a light apparatus furnished with hooks for holding the outdoor garments is slung up to the rafters, and hauled down at the dinner-hour and end of the shift—a contrivance similar to the airing apparatus in the kitchens of private houses, and in laundries. The slinging apparatus has the distinct advantage of putting garments beyond the reach of pilfering hands; for thefts sometimes occur in the Arsenal, but, considering the vast numbers and diverse population, the percentage of theft is small.

Still, it is undeniably one of the grievous results of war conditions that quite a number of people regard as legitimate the annexing of any property or material that is left about. This aspect has been noted in various hospitals, both in England and at the front; and I well remember, when in France, a chaplain saying to a young orderly: " My lad, if you can keep your hands off other people's property, you will have gained a great victory."

There are many checks to theft in the Arsenal. Shifting-houses are never left, and everyone is liable to be searched at any time

under duly authoritative orders. If a theft
occurs in any factory, and the fact is made
known to the gate policeman, anyone may be
stopped and searched before they leave the
Arsenal. And the gate search may take
place at any time, on entering or leaving.

Every woman worker in the Arsenal dons
overall and cap. In non-danger buildings,
khaki or blue overalls are given to newcomers ; at the end of the week they receive
a second, and are responsible for the washing
of cap and overall and keeping them in a fair
state of preservation. Every worker is known
by her factory number. It is stencilled on
her overall, not seldom accompanied by her
Christian name or a nickname.

In Danger Buildings the Shifting-house is
an elaborate organisation. On entry, each
worker takes off outer garments, jewellery,
metal fastenings, combs, and hairpins. All
property, all metallic adjuncts, must be discarded ; the only loose articles allowed to pass
over the barrier are a handkerchief and a small
linen money-bag tied round the neck.

The Shifting-house is a long building cut
into two by a barrier painted red. This barrier
runs across the entire width, and divides the

"dirty" side (*i.e.* the side of entry) from the "clean" side (*i.e.* the side from which the workers pass out to workshop). It is divided longitudinally into three, four, or more sections, according to the size of the factory, by wooden partitions, furnished with rows of numbered pegs. Each worker hangs her outdoor clothes on a peg on the "dirty" side, and has a corresponding peg on the "clean" side for her kit-bag, which contains Arsenal shoes, gown, and cap, and is stencilled with her number. Having hung up her clothing on the "dirty" side and placed her boots in the pigeon-hole below her peg, and delivered up attaché case and handbag, she advances to the barrier. There she undergoes a careful search by persons stationed at the barrier for this special duty. When the searcher is satisfied that no metallic fastenings, hairpins, jewellery are worn by the worker, and that the pockets are empty and sewn up, she is allowed to pass over the red barrier. She then dons gown, cap, and shoes, *if she can find them* ; but, too often for the D.P.O.'s peace of mind, she makes great lamentation over the loss of one article or of the entire kit.

For in every Shifting-house in the Arsenal

there is a Puck, a mischievous sprite who goes about between the shifts, taking a gown here, a cap there, sometimes putting two or three gowns into one bag; *but some bags he never touches.* I knew many workers who tied their kit-bags with care, and took some trouble to hang them on high pegs, and they seldom, if ever, lost their things. The girls, however, never put it down to Puck, but always to the Other Shift. This other shift was responsible, in their estimation, for everything that went amiss; and the other shift laid the blame of any untoward event to the girls of my shift.

"Oh, miss!" is a very common remark, "the other shift has taken my shoes again"; or, "Miss!" (tragically) "my *new* gown: the other shift has worn it, and it's quite black."

Enter the Shifting-house night or day at any moment between 6.50 and 7.15. A scene of wild disorder meets the eye. A sea of heads and writhing bodies, and apparently utter chaos. But order gradually resolves on the "clean" side, in the shape of tidy figures clad in creamy or brown gowns buttoned up to the neck and close to the wrists, with tightly-fitting caps which should conceal the

hair. But the girls who voluntarily hide
their hair beneath their caps are few in
number. Yet they looked quite charming
when the regulations were entirely followed
and my lasses of seventeen or eighteen appeared in cream-coloured gowns with not a
wisp of hair showing beneath their caps, like
sedate little nuns.

The Arsenal has its fashions in the way of
wearing a gown and the method of donning
a cap. The ingenuity of the feminine mind
is always in evidence in this respect in ways
both droll and delightful, and is one of the
methods of beguiling long and exacting hours
of work. The cap, which is merely a circular
piece of material with a tape run round the
edge, would trick the uninitiated into thinking
that there were at least a dozen different
shapes of caps.

There are fashions also in relieving touches
of colour. Flowers were used in the summer
and autumn. Certain workshops chose special
colours. Tiny blush-roses were a favourite in
one shop; yellow marguerites in another; in
a third, sweet peas. But it is the D.P.O.'s
duty to unbendingly repress such ebullitions
of ornament, for, being in Danger Buildings,

nothing must enter the workshops which is extraneous to the work. So throughout the summer and autumn she made " war upon the summer's velvet bud," confiscating these decorations and placing them with Shifting-house attendants, to be owned in the dinner-hour. The confiscation was generally effected without demur, by admiring the flowers, reminding the owner that nothing was allowed in the workshops; that flowers could be worn in the dinner-hour, when they could make themselves look festive if they pleased. And the flower was handed over to the D.P.O. with a smile and an assenting " I'm sure."

Since the wearing of flowers proved unsatisfactory, ribbon was the next innovation. It was cleverly introduced by exchanging the Government shoe-lace for ribbon. The fashion was introduced by the Cap Shop girls, who appeared one morning with bright emerald-green ribbon in their shoes. The other workshops in the factory looked upon this bold setting of the fashion with admiring and envious eyes, as the Cap Shop girls strutted about all that day, delightedly self-conscious, the most obvious part of their attire being the green ribbons in their shoes. The following morning

the whole factory was in the fashion. Shoes
were tied with blue, pink, red, white ribbon;
with anything but the Government boot-lace
of untanned leather. The fashion spread to
the office: the women clerks paraded the platform during dinner-hour with resplendent
shoe-laces. The attendants also followed
suit, and dear old Auntie Ellis,[1] the senior
attendant, and a great favourite with our
women, was discovered wearing shoe-strings
of bright scarlet, and in answer to the cry of
"How gay you are, Auntie!" she remarked
with a twinkle in her eye, "I'm wearin' the
Government's red tape; it's accordin'." These
shoe-strings had been procured from the strips
of waste which the Tailor's Shop used to tie
the gowns into bundles for delivery at our
factory. There was always a scramble to gain
possession of some of this "red tape" for girdles,
which was yet another method for the display
of fashion, and great were the efforts amongst
the workers to ingratiate themselves with
Auntie Ellis for this purpose. Auntie Ellis
was sworn henchman to the D.P.O. She had
a genius for contriving hiding-places for caps

---

[1] The Shifting-house attendant is always addressed as
"Auntie."

and money-bags, which the D.P.O. doled out to needy applicants at mid-day. And when she understood the difficulties of the gown question, she became a veteran in the art of keeping a few gowns for emergencies, taking charge of special overlookers' gowns, which by reason of their newness were liable to disappear either through the caprice of the sprite Puck, or by reason of the necessitous and impoverished "Other Shift."

And Auntie May, the other attendant, was an able aide-de-camp. Both were cheery and happy workers. They scoured the Shifting-house until it shone again. Always busy and dependable in their tasks, they were two of the best workers it was the D.P.O.'s good fortune to possess.

The Shifting-house is to the munition worker what the eighteenth-century coffee-house was to its generation, and more. It is the news-room, the reading-room, sewing-room, place for drinking tea (on the "dirty" side). And here the tired worker, after carefully balancing herself on a twelve-inch-wide bench, will sleep happily and dreamlessly until the hootah and the determined voice of the D.P.O. rouse her, sending her forth once more to the workshop.

Nowadays there are canteens and rest-rooms, but the women still look upon the Shifting-house as the home part of the establishment, especially in the older factories, where for some months it was their only shelter for meals and rest.

The D.P.O. is on duty during the dinner-hour to give passes for caps and gowns and money-bags, to listen to any personal matter, and to deal with permits for early leaving. Women who are soldiers' wives must have facilities for drawing their pay once a week, or a mother needs to take her sick child to hospital; there are parcels to send to relatives who are fighting or prisoners of war. These are legitimate cases for granting leave half-an-hour earlier, and these must be carefully sifted out from reasons which are not necessary. So the dinner-hour passes like a flash, as the D.P.O. deals with the small but numerous demands of her workers.

The rules are read in the Shifting-house on the first day of every month. They are daily explained to the newcomers, but the Danger Building regulations are so important that they are constantly recapitulated. How we all pack ourselves in is a marvel on these occasions! The D.P.O. mounts to a place of vantage whence she can view the sea of faces below her, with the overflow squeezed round the doorway and on the platform outside. The sensible take the rules with a shrug; the rebellious mutter " Rules again ! "; the incorrigible murmur amongst themselves until they are called to order; and all are reduced to respectful silence except an occasional laugh elicited by a facetious thrust from the D.P.O. And when it is over they hasten out once more, all talking at once, and saying to the D.P.O., " That's over for another month."

Lastly, the Shifting-house is the place where clean or new gowns are given: an event which lacks interest to the general reader; but to the Principal Overlooker the whole life and temper of the factory hangs upon the question of gowns. The overlooker, or head of each workshop, must be kept tidy. The filler's gowns must be changed often, because they soon become impregnated with powder. The mercury and compo workers need a weekly change as a preventative against contact, and every worker needs a fortnightly change.

Now, the desire and ambition of the factory

4

is to obtain a new gown; for the fireproof material is soft and glossy in appearance when new, but its colour changes to a brown shade and it loses its gloss when washed.

When new gowns arrive, the news speeds round the factory, and the majority suddenly discover that their gowns are dirty, or misfits. The D.P.O. is waylaid with breathless demands for new gowns. "Oh, miss, I've *never* had a new gown," says one; "I've been here four months and never had a new gown," says another; and a third says insistently, "You *promised* me one." "No," replies the D.P.O. to the last suppliant: "I never promise gowns, because I cannot regulate the supply. Like you, I must wait patiently, and distribute the gowns fairly in the order they are due, when I receive them." New gowns are supplied to overlookers and fillers only, as a rule. But when a large batch of gowns is sent, it is sometimes possible to clothe an entire shop in new gowns. The Tailor's Shop works night and day to make and renovate gowns, and the supply of washed gowns is adequate for the general worker. But there is no insistent demand for a washed gown; and the persuasion, even the command, of the

D.P.O. is required to effect a change from a dirty *new* gown to a clean washed one.

Thus a large portion of the D.P.O.'s energy is spent in administering gowns, selecting and rejecting, and adopting a system of impartiality in dealing with two hundred applications or more when there are forty or fifty to be distributed.

The workers beg, demand, beseech, according to their temperaments. One gently says she does not wish to worry, but . . . ; another affirms that she has waited long enough ; a third complains that the factory laughs at her patched gown ; and a fourth ingeniously requests a new gown because she is going to be married.

The only way to deal with our lasses is by infinite patience and good-humour, and discernment in selecting the deserving cases. Sometimes the D.P.O. exclaims : " These gowns of yours, lasses, will be the death of me ; if I don't appear one of these days, you will know that I have succumbed to the gowns."

" Oh, miss, we know it's not you," they reply in contrite tones. It is not to be wondered at that a few workers out of a number of five

hundred must wait their turn, considering we
are only one factory of many. The gown
supply became quite normal, and the marvel
is that the Tailor's Shop manages to meet
the great demand.

My girls are never so happy or look so
radiant as on the red-letter days when they
acquire new gowns. And their happiness is
completed with a new cap as well. How they
laughed when the D.P.O. visited them the
other day, when from force of habit two
girls jumped up saying, " Oh, miss ! may we
have a new gown ? " Two instances of real
self-sacrifice must be recorded. A worker
gave up a gown to someone who needed
it ; and another girl allowed a filler to have
the new gown which had just been assigned
to her.

In the New Year, the excitement of garbing
the carriers in a special rational uniform made
the general worker forget her attire for a time.
The women carriers appeared with belted overall reaching to the knee, gaiters fastened above
the knee, and divided skirt reaching below
the knee. Mackintosh overcoat and cap
completed the uniform. Very serviceable
and workmanlike these uniforms are, for the

carriers must be out in all weathers, and the ordinary length skirt and gown is not only an impediment, but a menace to health. It is now worn in parts of the Arsenal where women are employed as carriers or truckers.

Much has been said about Arsenal dress, because it is both the preparation and the precaution for the business in the workshop. Being suitably equipped, the workers leave the Shifting-house, and we will follow them to their respective workshops.

CHAPTER IV

THE WORKSHOPS : MORNING

" Man goeth forth unto his work and to his labour."
Psalter.

FROM 7.15 to 7.30 daily and nightly the
D.P.O.'s exert all their energy, all their force
of will, all their patience, and not a little of
their wit in getting the girls to their workshop.   The phrase, " Come along, girls," is
incessantly on their lips, the reiteration varied
only by the stress.   The command of the
D.P.O. is (literally) enforced by the driving
power of the attendants.   Auntie Ellis's voice
is heard : " Come along, you gals ; this way
for the up train," with a further admonish-
ment : " Now, then, what yer doin' up there
all of a heap ?—out you go."   So by dint of
continually calling and propelling, the house
is cleared by 7.30, and the door closed.

Once in the workshop, away from the
temptation to gossip, or snatch a forbidden

hasty meal on the dirty side of the Shifting-house, or to rest after the journey there, our women start work with energy. The out-going shift must leave the shops clean and tidy. It is the business of the incoming shift to set up and burnish all machinery and tools. On cleanliness depends our safety. The three commandments of the Danger Buildings are Cleanliness, Gentleness, Punctuality, and on these principles depend all the regulations. The first two ensure safety, the last speeds munitions to the front, and will shorten the war. These three words might be written large in every Shifting-house in Great Britain, to impress it on all workers, as we endeavoured to impress it on our lasses.

The most acutely busy time of the shift for the D.P.O. is from 7.30 to 8 o'clock. She goes swiftly from shop to shop, noting absen-tees and arranging the gangs of workers for the operations. The filling shops must be kept to their full strength. Vacancies in these shops entail drawing from minor operations, or appointing new hands. Discernment must be made between what is vital and what is expedient. One operation leads to another, and if we are held up in one direction, the

work as a whole is affected. Moreover, the
work of the previous shift must be balanced
by the following shift.

The foremen and D.P.O.'s are therefore
engaged, as it were, in a game of chess, the
factory being the board, the workers the
pawns, and the other shift the " friendly foe."
At the end of the week, when the exacting
work necessitates a rest for some of our
women, the volunteer workers are a great
boon, in keeping gangs up to strength and
preventing any lowering of the output.

It should be understood that workers are
safe, as long as they follow out instructions
and work to rule. Directions are printed in
every shop. It is the overlooker's duty to
see that the workers are following these
directions, and the D.P.O. must see that every
shop is working exactly in accordance with
such regulations. She must be constantly on
the alert to note any deviation whatever from
the directions, and to watch for danger signals.
She must be satisfied that the machinery is
running smoothly and correctly, and if in
doubt go to the experts. The men D.P.O.'s
supervise, correct, and adjust machinery, and
make constant tours of inspection. Still the

woman D.P.O. is responsible for the women, and she cannot relax a moment in watchful guard.

By 8 o'clock the filling machines must be up and running, the mould trays and plates must be thoroughly clean, the shop must have its complement of hands, the absentee lists must have been collected and signed by the D.P.O. and sent up to the office, and the programme of the day in working order.

On the night-shift work continues without a break until 11 p.m., the dinner-hour. On the morning shift dinner is at midday; and light refreshments are served in the canteen between 8 a.m. and 9 a.m. Every worker is allowed ten minutes: five minutes to go to the canteen and back, five minutes for refreshment. At 9 a.m. all stragglers are called in, the canteen is closed to workers, and inspection of workshops begins. The D.P.O. visits every shop, in more leisurely fashion than the first round. She watches the work, points out errors, notes the progress of new hands, inspects the supply of hypo and eye lotion and towels in the filling shops. The inspection is followed by a visit to the wash-houses and adjacent buildings, and to the Shifting-houses to see that everything is in a clean and sanitary condition. Lastly, reports are made, requisitions drawn up, and the ambulance baskets overhauled and depletions made good before the "turn-out" hootah sounds at midday.

Starting on our morning's rounds, we enter the Cap Shop. This is the largest shop in the factory; hence it appears to be the most busy. There is constant movement here, as the girl carriers go backwards and forwards with the plates for the different processes and operations, all of which are begun and completed in this shop.

The Cap Shop is always full of life. The girls sings their special Cap Shop songs and ragtime ditties. The row of merry faces round the star-turning table is one of the bright corners of our factory, while the bounces of bright-coloured shell add a touch of picturesqueness to the scene. It recalled to the memory a little fairy tale called the "Pot of Gold," describing the quest of a boy and girl for the golden treasure that was hidden at the foot of the sunset, and after many adventures they climb a mountain below which the sun is setting, and they fall asleep and dream they are laving their hands in

streams of gold. But the fairy tale is more
of an allegory; for every boy and girl, every
man and woman sets forth to find that
treasure, though some lose themselves by the
way. But those who search are so taken up
with the attractions on the road, and find such
glories on the mountain top when they have
scaled it, that almost before. they are aware
they near the sunset, and go down with it to
learn the glowing mystery of what shall be
revealed beyond. And sometimes, at different
crossroads, there are partings from friends; but
at every parting there is a trail of light, and a
bright spirit remains with them, more real than
the bodily presence they parted with, because
the body is merely the semblance of the spirit
and the soul.

The majority of the filling shops are staffed
with women. The mercury shops have men
overlookers, with women as second-in-charge.
The shops, divided in three portions, are not
large, owing to the nature of the operations,
but each worker in the shop has an important
process to carry out. These shops are remark-
able for the happiness and general appearance
of good health among the workers. Singing
is the usual accompaniment to their work.

The latest songs are introduced, but some songs which are rich in harmony remain favourites and are sung week in and week out with tireless energy. Carols were introduced for the Christmas season. " Noël " and " King Wenceslaus " were the favourites, and were sung with a spirit and tunefulness hard to beat, while the machinery made an undercurrent of rhythmic sound.

Many a time I have desired to sketch these workshops, but the limitations of perspective would only permit a portion to be seen; whereas it is the whole effect, the " tout ensemble " (as our friends across the water say) of rhythmic work and tuneful song that appeals to eye and ear. Though every filling shop is similar, each has its distinct characteristics to the initiated. The energetic overlooker of the —— shop was always wrapped up in his work, planning out the best possible arrangements of his workers, in order to add to the output, putting a machine in order at one moment, taking up a filling machine at another, giving a woman-pupil a lesson, making out attendance lists, talking over the work with the D.P.O.—never wasting a moment, and always engrossed in some plan ahead of the work. Foremost amongst those who help their comrades, he aided the Red Cross Fund with much zeal, and at the Christmas season subscriptions were given from his shop sufficient to buy an adjusting-table for the St John's Relief Hospital. The woman second-in-charge ably supported him, and the whole shop following the tone of their leader, were known for their good work.

The next shop to them worked in close unison and friendly rivalry. Where one was in advance, the other essayed to lead. The overlooker was formerly a sailor and kept his shop as taut and clean as a ship's deck. The shop was noted, too, for its enthusiastic women-in-charge. Little Miss C——, beloved by all the workers, was sunny, sweet-tempered, and absolutely loyal to work, but eye-trouble necessitated transfer to another factory, to our mutual regret. Her place was ably filled by another loyal worker, who inspired the girls under her to good work. She is now overlooker in another shop.

Another shop was conspicuous for the number of fillers it turned out. There was always a prospective pupil here, willing to

learn, and it had the honour of supplying
fillers for other shops. The overlooker was
a woman, supported by a man-filler of large
experience. The other fillers were women,
with a long record of steady work. There
was always in this shop a steady cheerfulness
in the face of obstacles. The overlooker was
ready to throw herself in the breach when
emergency arose. Hence she inspired her
workers, so that one saw a hand quietly going
from one operation to another if there was
any need, with no grumbling and no assertion
that "it wasn't their place" to help in the
operation required.

It was the aim of the D.P.O. to see that
the hands in filling shops should be capable
of turning from one operation to another.
In this way much time is saved, and the shop
is generally in a higher state of efficiency.

Another shop was distinguished for its
women-fillers, who had a very long record
at their work; and they were respected by
all the workers of the shop. One of these
has since become overlooker of the shop,
and she has the good wishes and support of
all, because we feel that she will make a loyal
and good leader.

On the first day of the New Year, we opened the half of a new filling shop with much eager interest. Thither we brought picked hands from the old shop, and some promising new hands. The shop famous for its fillers supplied a hand for the filling machine. But one thing was lacking, and the D.P.O. was asked with some diffidence if H—— were not coming down. Now H—— was a bonny lassie who had worked in the old shop for *eleven* months—ever since the shop had been open to women, in fact. For this reason she was an integral part of the shop, and we were dubious of removing her. But when the D.P.O. went to see, she was confronted with a wistful face, and a sorrowful voice begged to be allowed to go to the new shop. "Let me go as a worker," she said; "I do not wish to be second-in-charge, but just to be allowed to work there." My friends X, and Y, and Z are all there, and I shall feel more at home with them in the new shop." We sympathised, and felt that she deserved a reward. Twice during the eleven months her eyes had shown signs of trouble, and we wanted to remove her, but she had begged hard to remain, so we carefully watched her until the eyes became normal again.

We considered that her long service merited the reward she asked, so, having received the master's assent, we took H—— down to the new shop, triumphantly presenting her to the workers there, to the great contentment of all.

We paid a flying visit to this shop the other day, and found proudly happy faces. The work was pursued with great vigour to show us how well the shop was running. And the overlooker said in quiet tones: "All is well here; and next time you come to see us we hope to have the other half of the shop working."

The D.P.O. must keep a vigilant eye on the appearance of the workers during her daily rounds, noting especially the eyes and the skin, and inquiring into the state of teeth and gums. Experience has proved that careful watching and taking care of contact cases in the early stages has a most beneficial result. Some workers are better if left in the shop under surgery treatment; others, again, are better removed on the slightest symptoms. Some are immune, having remained for months without becoming contact. The preventative measures have greatly decreased the number of cases.' Hypo for the hands and face, and eye lotion are placed in every mercury and compo shop, and workers can stop their work to use these preventatives at any moment during the day. Increased accommodation for washing and hot and cold water laid on in the shops, together with the free distribution of milk at every shift, has done much to raise the general health of our workers.

From filling we pass to finishing. The operation needs delicate handling and skilled labour: deftness of touch and a trained eye are essential. The work is particularly adapted to women, and overlookers and hands are women and girls who have reached a very high standard of efficiency and dexterity. The overlookers of both the filling and the finishing shops must be thoroughly experienced. They need to be observant and resourceful, with a taste for machinery, and must, moreover, be swift and dexterous in manipulation.

There is always something new to learn, some fresh difficulty to cope with, some slight amendment to try; hence the work is absorb-

5

ingly interesting. The discs, their measurements, weight, thickness, and the variety of metal used, is a science in itself, as applied to the particular branch of work in these shops. The D.P.O. must watch closely, satisfying herself that the work is performed strictly to the printed rules of the shop. The total amount in a shop must never exceed a certain limit, and it must be constantly carried away.

The work of the Carriers is most important in relation to both the filling and the finishing shops. They carry away the finished work and supply the finishing shops with fresh work. All work must be removed as soon as it is finished, and it is often necessary to put an extra carrier on at busy times, when there is an increased amount to carry away. Detonator-carrier duty is popular amongst the women, and, now the carriers wear a rational uniform, they are prepared for all weather. They like the out-door life. A worker who has been suffering from contact with mercury often becomes quite well again under the out-door life: others again are so sensitive to mercury that the duties of a carrier immediately set up dermatitis, and they must be removed.

We finish our brief survey with the Examining Shops. The workers here are either permanent examiners as a reward for good service in mercury, and their subsequent contact with it, or they are mercury workers who are taking their weekly rest in the examining shop; the following week they will return to mercury, and other mercury hands will take their place for a week. It is hoped thereby to lessen the cases of contact, and the plan is working well. The examining shops are the quietest in the factory. Much responsibility devolves upon each worker; it is their duty to separate any imperfect or faulty specimen in the finished work brought to them. To pass a defective cap or detonator means the spoiling of a cartridge or a shell; the women know their obligation, and carry out the work with a gravity and quietude befitting their responsibility and the trust reposed in them.

At another examining shop the overlooker, Mr H——, cheerily greets us, and is ready to show us all flaws that it is possible to detect. This work is the most highly trained in the factory. All defects are put aside to be rectified if possible. The examined work is sent on to the official examining department, where it is again minutely examined and tested.

This shop employs picked workers only. Long service, good records, and special ability for the work is essential. Women are placed here, as a rule, in reward for past services, and it is one of the best-paid operations.

Morning inspection is not complete until Shifting-house and the various offices have been visited. Bright rows of taps and well-scrubbed boards meet the eye in the wash-houses. At the door of the Shifting-house a strong smell of disinfectant is noticeable. At the call of " Mrs Ellis," an answering voice replies, " Here I am, miss, on my knees agin," and a cheerful figure emerges from a dark corner whence a moment before sounds of scrubbing were heard. A hasty survey, and a talk about supplies of gowns and shoes, a glance into the medicine cupboard to see that it is well stocked, and it is time to return to the platform for the turn-out.

Standing at a point of vantage on the bridge where the shops can be surveyed, the foremen and D.P.O.'s watch the workers as they stream out, at the sound of the hootah, to their dinner and well-earned rest.

CHAPTER V

AFTERNOON IN THE FACTORY

> " As with the morn
> The busy hours fly on, till afternoon
> Fades into night."—*Anon.*

THE settling of the workers after the dinner-hour is not quite such a strenuous business as the morning routine. The changes are slight, the absentees few. There is time to note natural effects which we are so fortunate in possessing. The workshops stand far apart on their own small grass plots, where an occasional tree casts cool shadows in hot weather, and their bare branches in wintry seasons add a touch of beauty to an otherwise barren landscape. The girls work away all the afternoon in fine weather with the wide doors flung open in view of the grass plots. When our workers are transferred they realise more than ever their good fortune in having belonged to our factory. " Oh, miss," they come to tell us, " I wish I

were back here; the work's all right in the
——— factory, but it's not the same as ours,
not 'arf!" However, the preference for their
own factory is not peculiar to our girls. Visiting others, I found the same (proper) spirit in
them. "Of course," one would say in a com-
miserating tone of voice of regretful patron-
age, "your shaped buildings are on the old
design. We are delighted with our picturesque
style, and are glad to be in one of the new
factories." We admired the buildings, adding
thoughtfully, "But we in our factory have our
glimpses of water, and sometimes see those
tawny-coloured sails floating past. . . ." The
subject was hastily changed, each one smiling
at the humour underlying the other's point
of view.

Pacing the platform on a fine afternoon,
there were many little corners of the original
marsh ground almost untouched. In one
quiet corner, for example, was a small plot of
reeds and flowery grasses. Just such a place
that Pan delighted in and made sweet music
from the reeds he plucked from the river side.
There were dragon-flies too, and water-beetles:
nor was bird-life wanting, for the trees scattered
over our area harboured hosts of sparrows:
sparrows who were tame enough to lodge in

the canteens; and it was a customary sight
for a sparrow to fly in and hop about the
canteen floor, picking up crumbs with non-
chalance like that of the pigeons at the
British Museum.

Fringing the ditches and on the mounds
between the shops, flowers were plentiful in
summer and autumn.   The small yellow antir-
rhinum covered some slopes near our Shifting-house; wild geranium, marsh daisies, and
many herbs were plentiful; and in the winter-
time two mounds were covered with bright
crimson berries which had ripened from a small
creeping plant, which had established itself
firmly in this particular spot.

The ditches have their colour effects, for
here the waste of chemicals and steam pipes
collect—great splashes of indigo variegated
with the rainbow tints, sometimes taking
strange shapes similar to the weird designs of
the Futurist school so prevalent before the
war.   And I often thought they must have
based their designs on the gorgeous effects
which masses of water take on when certain
chemical combinations are introduced, though
in applying the principle to an art they seemed
to lose all the natural beauty of the original
designs.

The clothing of the boys often adds a richness to colour effects. Small figures are to be seen on the platforms clad in trousers and cap of a rich velvety bronze brown; some of them possess features not unlike the cherubs of the Sistine Madonna, and one exclaims, "Oh, had we a Raphael or Angelo here, what colours, what gestures would be fixed for all time!"

Everyone knows that the cherubs of the Sistine Madonna gazing upwards adoringly were an inspiration, an afterthought of Raphael, on seeing two little Roman urchins looking up from the foot of the scaffolding to gaze upon the "Madonna and Bambino," then nearly completed.

There exists in the factory many such chubby-faced boys with glowing eyes and sunny countenance, their hair ruffled with work, who in picturesque garments bend lithe arms and bodies to their machines, whose behaviour, alack! often belies their seraphic expression. One day I found such a youngster in a filling shop, where his duty consisted of putting empty shell into the moulds. He was the picture of health, being the living counterpart of Greuze's "Child with the Apple"; and the likeness was only too complete, for he was munching with intense enjoyment a large rosy apple.

Oh, that apple ! A very stringent rule forbids " any eating whatever, except in certain appointed places." This rule refers to all ranks whatsoever. Enjoyment gave place to fear when I sternly demanded the apple and questioned him about the rule, made, like every other rule, for the safety of the whole factory. After a talk I told him that I should not report him now, but should expect him to help me in keeping the rules from henceforth. We made our compact and kept it. The lads knew that the D.P.O. allowed no wavering in the matter of rules, and was known to be overstern in this respect, than otherwise. From that day, the boys of my shops were always helpful, and willing in various ways. The boys were not controlled by the Women Principal Overlookers, but they liked to be included in any schemes we planned for the women, and smiles of welcome and cheery salutes were always ready when we met them in workshop or platform.

In the afternoon we visit the workshops on the other side of the factory. The X shop overlooker is an expert with a vast knowledge of his subject, and is always completely absorbed in the science and interest of it, and in the arranging of the women workers according to their ability. His ideal is to make his workshop perfect in technique, and the quantity of his output correspondingly satisfactory. Many a pleasant half hour was spent in getting initiated into the variety of operations in the shop, and in learning to know the girls.

The usual routine of visiting and inspecting is varied in the afternoon by visitors in an official capacity. The D.P.O. conducts the women M.O.'s and Welfare Visitors on tours of inspection, reporting and explaining by the way. These visitors generally exclaim at the cheerfulness and well-being of the shops, and we reply that everyone is happy, and owing to the many preventative measures adopted, they are usually very well. It took some time to get these measures into smooth working order, and it was a proud moment when our M.O., paying a flying visit, said, " I really have nothing to criticise to-day : your workers are in excellent health, to judge by their appearance. and your arrangements are in good working order." We both understood that this report did not mean any relaxation in watchfulness. It is only unflagging attention and continual insistence upon the use of preventative measures, and the hourly inspection of shops, that keep in abeyance the number of contact cases, and improve the health of the workers. Unflagging interest and continual care are the two watchwords of the D.P.O.'s.

A few minutes before the hootah sounds for tea, we must be on the platforms, and at the observation post. For if no foremen or D.P.O.'s are about the factory considers it has scored in turning out too soon. Therefore, whatever happens, the D.P.O.'s must be at their posts to see that order is kept. The overlookers are responsible for their workers, and any laxity in this respect means severe reprimand. The D.P.O. gives the signal to the overlookers, and each overlooker turns the shop out at leaving time. Great watchfulness must be observed to keep order on the platform : haste is firmly repressed, for no running is allowed on danger platforms. Every worker, however, wishes to get to canteen or Shifting-house as quickly as possible, so all the officials are on the alert at different parts of the factory to see that this rule is observed.

After tea the shops are visited, and absentees noted. The remaining hour or two is occupied with technical details. The D.P.O.

generally repairs to the office which is jointly shared by men and women, between the hours of five and six o'clock, to make out reports for the Principal Foremen, and bring the surgery list and absentee lists up-to-date. Any small points of adjustment in organisation are notified to the following shift. A last visit is made to the workshops, to see that all is in order before the leaving hootah sounds; and we found that this was a good time, when other points of routine did not claim attention, to ascertain whether the workers were in receipt of their correct shares, and to note the day's changes in the occupations of the women.

When the workers have once again streamed out, and are safely in the Shifting-houses, it is necessary to visit the X and Y shops, to see that they are left clean, and that nothing is remaining in them contrary to regulations. Then comes the summing up of the day. The woman meets the men P.O.'s, and the day's work is totalled up and discussed: suggestions made for improvement here, correction there, in work or worker. The men overlookers generally come in to give their verbal report and discuss the difficulties and successes of the day.

And now the platforms, that were so silent during the previous half hour, begin to hum with life. Overlookers of the night-shift are hurrying to their shops; workers are strolling leisurely to their various occupations, chatting as they go. It is nearly 7.30 and time to leave, so we exchange Arsenal for outdoor shoes, and have a word with the D.P.O. of the night-shift before our departure.

Once out of the factory, we realise that we are hungry and weary. If the night is fine and starlit, there is solemnity and peacefulness in the walk through the now quiet Arsenal. Walking along the way that teemed with many thousands and resounded to the tramp of hurrying footsteps but a short while since, we revolve in our minds the various incidents of the day, and realise the comic side of some event that at the time of happening obliged an attitude of gravity, if not of sternness.

Scrutinised by sentinel and policeman, but unmolested, we at length reach the gates that we entered at 6 a.m., sufficiently thankful for space to walk in, and a seat in a tram. So we look forward on our homeward way to the cheery chat of friends at the dinner-table, and beyond that, repose.

CHAPTER VI

SLIGHT SKETCHES

"Sondry folk by aventure yfalle
In felaweshipe."   CHAUCER.

LEST the reader should have fallen into the grievous error that the D.P.O. is in supreme command, we would note that after the All-powerful Head comes the Controller, in charge of groups of factories; the Manager, responsible for a single group; the Principal Foreman, head of one or more factories, and the foreman of a single factory. Latterly, women foremen have been appointed, but in our time the D.P.O. was directly responsible for the women, and whatever appertained to them.

The Manager of our group of factories was a man of over middle height, blue-eyed and of ruddy complexion, as courteous a gentleman as one could wish to meet in a day's march. An optimist and believer in ideals, he main-

tained that to do good work it was necessary
to start with the aim of reaching one's ideal.
He has a way of listening to, and giving
decision upon a question of the women's
organisation as if it were of the most vital
importance, giving the matter his whole attention ; but before leaving the table, when the
interview is over, the face has already settled
into grave lines of thought, and the eyes are
looking into space, over some vast question
of importance with far-reaching effects. The
secret of his success lies in his power to
grapple and deal with large issues, together
with a belief in the importance of detail—
two qualities that are seldom found together.
Possessed with clear vision and straight aims,
he gives the lead to those under him, and they
are encouraged by the knowledge that what
he expects of others he first of all carries out
himself.

The Master is long-limbed and lean of body,
grey-eyed and square of jaw, his clean-shaven
face allowing every line of his purposeful
and determined character to be in evidence.
Yet the stern lines of his face can relax at
times into the kindliest of smiles, and with
a rare faculty of understanding points of view
which differ from its own, he shows a sympa-

thetic insight into the difficulties that underlie
all work that is honestly shouldered. He
can, moreover, detect with unerring exactness
that which savours of slackness or want of
straightness.

His energy drives an undertaking through,
which others might find too difficult or prob-
lematic to achieve. He puts all his power
into the need of the moment, all his resourceful energy into the exigencies of a particular
experimental operation. His own energy acts
as the driving power, the electric spark to
those who work under him ; and more than
once a brilliant inspiration has carried an
experiment to a successful conclusion, resulting in an increase of facility, with a minimum
of danger, to the special operation under in-
vestigation.

A word of censure from the Master is not
lightly regarded ; his rare word of praise
immeasurably elates. He has the respect
of all who work under him, and we never
approach him concerning any problem on the
welfare of the women without satisfaction as
far as it is possible.

There was also a worthy man called "Charles."
He had seen service in the Arsenal for some
five-and-forty years, and knew its constitution

and its foibles. A somewhat shrewd character was masked by a benevolent countenance, and still further softened by a fund of humour that welled up in the grey-blue eyes, and twinkled out as the precursor to some droll story reminiscent of Arsenal life of yesterday. His method of criticism was "to point a moral and adorn a tale." He combined this accepted twofold method in such a way, however, as to leave his audience in delighted enjoyment of the humour, with a fine disregard of the moral to be drawn.

He was the most popular element in the factory with our workers, and they lived in a state of expectation for a good ancedote whenever he came amongst them. A favourite way of preparing a reprimand was by asking and answering the following question : " My lads " (he generally addressed us in this way by force of long habit)—" my lads, what is it that consti-tutes a gentle-man ? Do as you would be done by." (Each syllable of the answer well emphasised). Reprimand would follow, concluding with an ancedote, providing the matter were not too grave. But at times both twinkle and ancedote were absent, and not until he left the shop, with the workers greatly subdued by this deliberate

6

omission, did the genial humour flash out again.

Promotion took him from us, to the regret of all, and we hear that he is rapidly becoming as popular in the new factory as he was in the old.

We had a shipman in our company also, who supervised machinery. He was very quiet and retiring, but always at hand to give substantial help when needed, in an unostentatious manner. His gravity was partly the result of great experience, having travelled and seen life in every part of the world, and partly a dislike of the glamour and noise of publicity. He had a quiet humour and could tell a good tale with great enjoyment in the rare moments when amenities of life were possible, for he was, as a rule, deep in the management of his machinery. We were fortunate in having his services on the night-shift during the long winter watches, when his quiet helpfulness was welcome on more than one occasion.

The senior Principal Overlooker on the day-shift was the great chess-player, with the factory as the board, and the workers the pawns. From morning till late at night he was arranging his pieces, and always with the utmost good temper. He was one of the hardest workers in the factory, yet always had time to explain a problem to the less initiated. However busy he might be, he switched off his mind in the dinner-hour on to the topics of the day and our position in the field of war, eagerly scanning the papers and commenting on the events. The junior P.O. was generally his companion at these times, and it was interesting to hear their views and ideas of life. Both were sincere and kindly. The junior P.O.'s work lay in the same direction as ours for some weeks, and he was always the same ; with a liking for fair dealing, he was very helpful in giving his opinion on points of factory organisation, and it was with real regret that we parted when our work lay in different directions.

Typical characters included the Scotch lady. One of the early workers in the Arsenal, she was promoted to our factory as P.O. on the other shift, and speedily became popular for her bonnie face and merry smile, besides a rare capacity for the manifold duties required of her. My women have said at times, " Oh, miss ! it does you good to look at her." And certainly she seemed to bring into the factory with her a breath of her own moors. She was, latterly, promoted to the office of forewoman, and well deserved the honour for her length of service and her physique, which carried her triumphantly through work and weather of all sorts. She is now in France.

The P.O. of her shift was a lady with a heart of "gold." Very clever in household management, she brought all her skill to bear on Shifting-house and dining-room administration. Her great ambition is to achieve a scheme for a perfect Shifting-house, where there will be no lost gowns or kits, and where order shall everlastingly reign. When we left she was still planning for a millennium. It was a continual pleasure to have her on the other shift; for it is this spirit alone, a determination not to be baffled, and ability to devise schemes, that will eventually bring about the highest measure of success possible.

The Water Carriers were familiar figures on the platforms. One large motherly person, about the size of three ordinary women, made a most excellent police-woman at the barrier, as nobody could possibly get past her without notice. Her companion was a short, stout, merry woman, who was never happier than when she was scrubbing.

The two special carriers of my shift were thoroughly dependable good workers. They supplied the shops with hypo and lotion, filling up their time with cleaning; their rows of burnished taps and well-scrubbed floors were always a welcome sight during the morning's inspection.

And to conclude our "celebrities," there was Auntie Ellis. She made the Shifting-house a home for our girls. She combined affection with a very fine wit, being the embodiment of the Shakspearean type of nurse, and carried the likeness to a startling degree by the use of Shakspearean epithets. She was untiringly ready at every demand for caps, shoe-strings, and tape. " Now, Cock," she would say to one lass, "what are you waiting for? Clean cap? You had a clean cap yesterday. D'you think the Government put me here to give you a clean cap every five minutes. You go away." But the girl receives a piece of stuff for a girdle to send her away happy. "What" (to another), "you want a new gown? Where's the P.O.'s order?" "Oh, the P.O. said I might have one," says the girl airily. "No!" says Auntie Ellis, "I'm not givin' any gowns without the P.O.'s order." At that moment the P.O. enters and the girl retires with discomfiture. Presently another worker enters with a beaming face and a signed order.

"A new gown, Auntie: a *new* one, mind."
"All right, matey," replies Auntie; "now
you're goin' to be fine." She suffered from a
troublesome cough in the winter, and when
asked how it was, she used to say, "Oh! I'll be
shot of it soon. You wait till Sunday: my man
will look after me, and I'll do fine." We shall
all remember, I think, in years to come, the
homely corner of that Shifting-house brightened
by the motherly person of Auntie Ellis, clad
in neat black gown, which, when tucked up
for scrubbing, revealed a fine purple petticoat,
and Arsenal shoes tied with the Government
"red tape." A purple knitted jacket completed her attire at about four o'clock, when the
work and the scrubbing were done; and with
smoothed-down hair and general tidied-up-ness,
one would hear her crooning an old ballad
while she assisted Auntie May to get their
cup of tea before the shift turned out.

CHAPTER VII

WOMAN'S WORK OUTSIDE OUR FACTORY

> " Here work enough to watch
> . . . and catch
> Hints of the proper craft, tricks of the tool's true play."
> BROWNING.

OUR factory is but one of a group of Danger Buildings, fronting moor and marsh, with the complexity of the Arsenal labour city behind us.

Contiguous to our buildings is the Cartridge Factory, with which we share a canteen. The Cartridge Factory employs many thousands of girls. Here, in a series of workshops, the caps turned out by the factory are deftly placed by hand into the cartridge cases; so swift and dexterous is the operation that the only approach to it is the play of a Chinaman's chopsticks as he picks up grains of rice. This work is paid by the piece, so that the more dexterous a girl becomes the more she earns.

The machinery used here is interesting.

Streams of cartridges pass along a narrow gangway, and get filled in the process. They then make a circular tour on round trays, and at a particular point, each cartridge has a bullet inserted which falls from a groove above into the neck of the cartridge below; then it passes on to the finishing stages. At intervals along these workshops are the gaugers and examining tables.

The final stages of packing and trucking are carried out in adjoining shops, This factory is a busy hive of incessant labour: the work is emphasised by the combination of sound. The noise of the machinery mingles with the clatter of cartridges as box after box is turned out. The decisive click of each cartridge as it falls from the filling machine, and the chatter of the girls dominated by the orders of overlookers, all make up a vast volume of sound.

The non-danger factory that supplies the cartridge cases is some distance away, near the gates, and is one of the largest workshops in the Arsenal. This huge shop has rows, or "streets," as they are technically called, of machines worked by girls. Every ten or fifteen machines has an overlooker; the operations are cartridge cases and bullets. Every street is supplied with fitters and tool-setters. There are many women tool-setters, and their numbers are on the increase. Women who show special ability for machinery—and it is interesting to learn what a number of women have a special aptitude in this direction—are taught the work. Some tool-setters, again, are university students specialising in science or mathematics.

Close at hand is another vast workshop, where cases are made for the filling factories. One of the chief operations here is the making of the fuse. Some of the finest machinery in the Arsenal is employed for the fuse head. After the first process of roughing out, the many operations are performed on one machine of shaping and inserting the thread. This wonderful machine has a central mechanism, and by a spoke of the wheel the fuse is brought into position on the one machine for every succeeding operation, when the previous one is completed. The machines are clean and shining. and the women are thoroughly proud of them, and realise their good fortune in having such interesting work. Every part of the operation must be most carefully tested, and the fuse must be correct to the $\frac{1}{1000}$ part of an inch. In these case shops there is generally some rivalry, more or less friendly, between fitter and worker, or gauger and worker. Workers don't like the gaugers to find mistakes in their work; this makes them exceedingly careful in their own gauging, for they endeavour to make sure that the work is true to gauge before it leaves their hands.

As for the Fitter, he is, as it were, a race apart. The fitter maintains that *some*body must set the machine, whereas *any*body can run it. But it is mostly bantering, and helps to pass the hours away, while both fitter and worker know in their hearts that both are needed; both are carrying out important work, and each is wanted. The fitters have their special corners in the workshop, and their own attitude towards life in general and the workshop in particular, but as a rule they graciously unbend, and are very helpful indeed.

Recently a wag of the Arsenal compiled a humorous set of laws called the Fitter's Ten Commandments. I quote the Tenth, with acknowledgments to the compiler: "Thou shalt not covet thy fitter's job, nor his wage, nor his beer, nor the hours of rest that are his."

A machine won't work, and the fitter says, "She's obstinate to-day" (a machine, like a ship, is feminine): "just like a woman, won't

go unless she wants to." And we keep
golden silence for eloquent reply, merely
glancing round this gigantic workshop with its
many thousand machines tended by women
and girls "all wanting to." And the fitter,
having heard the reply which is shouted in his
ear through the golden silence, smiles, and the
machine goes on again " wanting to " like all
the others.

Oh! in a vast shop like this with its " street "
upon " street " of machinery, we realise faintly
what it all means. Women who have seen
their men go forth are close behind them,
putting themselves into the breach for any
work that is to be done, realising, at first dimly,
and by degrees fully, the glory of patriotism
even to the dying for one's country. And not
only munition workers, nurses, women on land
service, but the women in the home tending
their children and nursing their babes are no
less in the van, for these children are the
citizens of to-morrow, the men and women
who will take their part in service for the
Empire when these dread times shall have
passed away, and our land shall have come
through the ordeal of suffering and learning, and
emerged wiser, happier, cleaner than before.

It is worth while glancing at the self-feeding

machines for making the screws for the fuse.
Brass rods of various diameters pass along,
insert themselves into the mouths of their
respective machines, are bitten off in certain
lengths, pass through the machines, and are
cut; shaped, and threaded on the way, and
finally drop out` into receivers as screws of
various sizes.

We were loth to leave this fascinating shop.
At the lower end of the building were the
gaugers' tables; and the assembling tables,
where the parts of the fuse are put together
after very careful testing. The forewoman,
Mrs H——, who spent some hours in most
kindly conducting me through the factory,
was an eloquent guide, having a thorough
technical and practical knowledge of each
machine. She was specially distinguished as
having entered the Arsenal for mechanical
training in the autumn of 1915, before women
had received any appointment there, and she
was among the first to be appointed. She is
now one of the Lady Superintendent's most
able lieutenants.

The fuse case, when complete, is sent on to
the filling factory, whither we may follow it to
a factory near ours. Arriving at the women's
Shifting-house, we receive a pair of overshoes,

and find ourselves in one of the oldest factories. The workshops open off very high platforms, giving the factory an appearance of a Swiss village, for snow was everywhere, and the workshops were raised high from the ground. We passed through the Dissembling Room, where the fuse is taken to pieces, and proceeded to view the various operations of filling. It is a very complex business, and varies according to the different type of fuse.

.   .   .

Passing over the communicating bridge leading from the platforms to the —— Factory, we found ourselves on more accustomed ground. Here the platforms were about two feet from the ground, and the workshops were very far apart, with wide spaces of green plots between. Seeing a woman's figure in the distance and making sure she was the P.O., we hailed her, much to her astonishment. Hurrying over the intervening space we showed our credentials and were welcomed by her. " I've met you at the right moment," said she, " for I'm just going round the shops, and it might have taken some time to find me had you come later." So we made the tour together. Shell-filling is the main occupation. We passed through the packing and loading shops, viewing with awe an enormous shell just completed and waiting to be trucked. Then we inspected a series of shops engaged in shell-filling, all done by women. In another set of shops were men and women engaged in a special part of the filling operation.

.   .   .   .   .   .

It is astonishing to see the ease with which the women lift the shells. We tried to lift a 35-pounder without success, until we were shown how to lift after the style of levering. Women can lift a 60-pounder single-handed. They were very anxious to show us the art of lifting shells, and seemed proud to do it. Then one woman, who acted as spokesman for the others, said, " Please don't forget to say that we lift our own shells," and they lifted them off and on the bench with an ease only learnt by long practice. It is certainly heavy labour, but women of strong build are employed here, and they enjoy the work.

It was in this factory that it was said, " A miss is as good as a man," for the women lift and manage, single-handed, shells up to 60-pounders. It takes two men to lift a 120-pounder, so that " a woman is at least as good as one man," it was laughingly averred. As usual, we find the girls and women thoroughly happy and contented, and there was thorough good fellowship between the men and women workers.

Time had sped: it was nearly dark, and bitterly cold. My guide, Mrs K——, insisted upon giving me a cup of tea, and we spent a happy half-hour together, chatting over various details of organisation, and finding it most helpful to have the experience of a P.O. from another factory. I wished then that the P.O.'s could manage to meet sometimes; it would be helpful. The difficulty is the arranging any time, as every moment is occupied when on duty.

I wished Mrs K—— good-bye, promising to come again, and hoping to meet her on some later occasion. The wind nearly swept me off the platform, an event to be carefully avoided, since, according to regulations, the ground is "dirty," and the person who leaves the platform and lands on the ground must wait until fresh shoes and overall is provided before she can climb on to the platform again. The bridge was reached in safety, however, and the Shifting-house gained, the overshoes returned to the overseer, and arrangements made to visit another factory.

The next morning the roads were impassable owing to a heavy fall of snow. But the morning after we ventured forth to the firing ground, in the face of a biting north-east wind, and melting snow which was fast turning to a sea of mud. Attired in high boots, short skirt, and coat buttoned up round throat and ears, we reached our destination, and found the assistant foreman superintending the arrangements for firing various forms of explosives. We were taken to a fireproof hut, where a very welcome fire was burning in a stove in one corner, and a small window set in the thick wall allowed a good view of the operation. The hut might have been a backwoodsman's hut in the far West; it contained merely the rudiments of furniture, in the shape of a small table, chair, and high bench, one or two cooking utensils, and a kettle slung by the stove, and round the wall on pegs were various articles of storm clothing, coats, mackintoshes, and caps, and in two corners of the hut top-boots. The wildness and solitariness of the marshes outside, and the roughness of the hut, suggested a locality far from England. But the hut was friendly and warm, and the preparations outside most interesting.

We were going on to lunch at a canteen near the gates, where three of our friends were running it. The assistant foreman walked part of the way with us along the pedestrian platform in the Broadway. A remark on types of character disclosed the fact that he was a Dickens' lover, and we chatted about his works. Our guide recited passages of his favourite *Martin Chuzzlewit*, which he was in the habit of reading to his wife in moments of leisure. The marshes reminded me of parts of *Great Expectations*; and we noted that many of Dickens' characters, which appear sometimes over-characterised to the uninitiated, may be found, to the life, in the Arsenal at this moment. One remembered that Dickens, in the early part of his career, had worked in a factory, and many of his characters were doubtless the result of that experience.

CHAPTER VIII

TROTYL WORKERS, TRUCKING, AND THE TAILOR'S SHOP

" J'ai plus de souvenirs que si j'avais mille ans."
                                    CHARLES BAUDELAIRE.

One sunny morning in the New Year, after a heavy fall of snow, we started on a visit to the trotyl workers. Under a blue sky the world lay white and glistening. Our way led past the old Plumstead Church and a footbridge across the marshes. A few minutes' walk brought us to the —— Gate. Crossing another footbridge we were once more in the Arsenal, and a few yards further brought us to our destination at the Shifting-house.

We were expected, and shoes were awaiting us. We were soon on the platform, where we found the Medical Principal Overlooker looking out for us. This factory is one of the largest and newest in the Arsenal, and is staffed almost entirely with women. Besides the manager, foreman, and assistant foreman, there are only a few expert workmen here. A large staff of forewomen and Principal Overlookers carry out the supervision and organisation of the women. There are three sections of P.O.'s : first, women who are responsible for the output ; secondly, those acting as medical P.O.'s ; thirdly, those who are responsible for Shifting-houses and gowns, and details more or less domestic. Through kindly guidance we were conducted through a series of workshops standing far apart from one another.

We arrived at an auspicious moment, for the medical P.O. was making her rounds, distributing the green veils, about which we had heard much and had long wished to see.

The interest, however, lay in the faces behind those veils, and in the hands so busily employed all day, or all night, long.

The trotyl shops are small. On entering one sees a table on either side of the doorway. Each table has six or seven workers, wearing green veils, which are fastened round their fireproof caps. Fire-proof gowns are buttoned from throat to hem, and fastened at the wrists. All wear respirators. The worker at the head of each table has scales in front of her. Three women work at either side of each table with small wooden boxes before them containing the trotyl powder.

Every bag is examined before it leaves the shop, and again when it reaches the packing shop. All loose bags are returned to the respective shops that issued them. The good bags are packed, and after labelling and dating are disposed of by the truckers. Some are taken to the shell-filling workshops in the factory; others are sent off for transit outside.

Careful observation and research for preventatives, and remedies against ill effects of trotyl upon the workers, have done much for their amelioration. As in the mercury, measures are largely preventative. The care of the health, good, freshly cooked food for the midday meal, the drinking of milk which is given to workers, and the use of disinfectants for hands and face, all contribute to the decrease of trotyl cases. Moreover, the same plan is adopted that we inaugurated in mercury, of giving workers a few days' rest on another operation after a spell in trotyl. The workers in C.E. have the same operation to perform as those in trotyl, but there is less liability to contact. Yet some workers are immune from trotyl and are highly sensitive to C.E. Others, again, can work in C.E. and are highly sensitive to trotyl. The same experience was noted at our factory. Compo hands were highly sensitive to mercury, and some mercury hands became contact in compo. Hence we early devised the plan of keeping compo and mercury workers quite distinct, and not sending our women promiscuously to compo or mercury. By keeping the two classes apart we gained very considerably in our shift.

The trotyl workers are noticeable for their high spirits and their merry faces. Some workers showed signs of dermatitis; others had complexions varying between pale lemon colour and deep gold, but the majority looked thoroughly healthy. When removed from trotyl, the skin soon regains its normal appearance, and the use of a special lotion supplied to the shops helps in a great measure to counteract the effect of trotyl upon the skin.

One bright-faced girl said, as we paused in one of the shops, " Do you see how I'm wearing my veil, miss ? " Indeed, I had already observed that she was wearing it twisted carelessly round her neck, and her face was uncovered. But the P.O. smiled, saying, " Oh, she is quite immune ; she has been in it for months, and nothing hurts her." And the girls laughed gaily, regarding it as a great triumph for this particular shop to have, as it were, a mascot amongst them.

There is something curiously uplifting, moving about these small shops chatting with the workers, while their busy hands move ceaselessly amongst the powder and the bags, they are so merry and light-hearted, and appear so happy in their work. They go on filling these bags day after day, in thousands, and many hundreds of thousands, while the ceaseless stream passes on, and there is always need for more. Bidding the workers good-bye, I told them that I should have liked a photograph of them wearing their veils and respirators, if that had been possible, but I should carry with me the unforgettable impression of the brightness of the life in their workshop, a sketch set in tones of yellow and green.

In my small experience of Arsenal life I had found that the British lass, like the British lad at the front, is ever the lighter-hearted as the work is the heavier or more risky.

We paid a visit to the Sewing Shop. It was arranged on the same lines as a linen store of a Military Hospital, having parallel partitions filled with deep shelves down the length of the shop, leaving corridors between for gangways. Here is stored all the woven material used for the various processes of the factory, besides being the workshop for cutting out, making, stamping, and dating, the supply of trotyl bags in the various sizes required.

Shell-filling is another operation; but we did not stay long here, as time had sped, and we had already viewed the process under Mrs K——'s guidance in the X˙ Factory; moreover, we were anxious to spare a few minutes to watch the truckers at their work.

Trucking is an important part of the work in this factory, for the shops are spread over a large area. Consequently, a large number of women are engaged in trucking.

Their dress is similar to that of our carriers, consisting of tunic over a divided skirt, leggings reaching about the knee, and mackintosh coat and cap. We constantly met the truckers about the platforms, and we noted some picturesque groups. One in particular consisted of five truckers round a trolley, their black waterproof coats smeared with patches of red where they had come in contact with the paint on shell or case in the process of hauling and trucking. Three were busy about the steering gear; the remaining two were leaning, one on either side of the trolley, and bending forward with hands lightly resting on the boarding. These figures, set in a background of glittering snow-covered roofs and platforms, made a vivid picture, enhanced by the smiling faces of the truckers, who were glowing with their exertions and the exhilaration of the frosty air. As we lingered, noting the details, my guide said, " You must see the truckers after lunch."

The factory was already moving out for the midday meal. We had lunch at the New Canteen, and our after-lunch coffee in the Principal Overlookers' rest-room, where those who were off duty assembled to rest, chat, or write letters. After a short rest in a most comfortable lounge chair, we set forth again to see the factory enter and pick up tickets.

We then turned to a point of vantage to see the truckers start. They moved off in a long line to their various destinations for loading up, their trucks painted white with lines of red, while some were merely trolleys. The trucks and trolleys are loaded up; the cases for transit outside are brought to the railway loading shed; the others go to various destinations in the factory.

Trucking is hard work. Heavy weights must be hauled and lifted. Women of stout build and strong muscles are chosen. The

life is thoroughly healthy, and their rational
dress protects them in all weathers.   The
truckers looked the picture of good health,
and their happy faces bore testimony to their
enjoyment of the work.

Trucking and shell-lifting are two examples
of hard work done by women, which at the
beginning of the war did not seem suitable.
But, as the need has arisen, women have
generally and steadily applied themselves to
tasks which had to be done.   There is very
little work that has not been experienced by
women, and done effectively and efficiently.
The sudden accession of strength for the task
has certainly become apparent, because of the
will to do it, the need for women to do the
work.   Yet it should be remembered that
in certain classes women have always known
what hard labour is.   The women who have
been obliged to wash and mangle and scrub
for their own families or in service, know all
that is to be learnt of hard labour.   The
number is pitifully large, too, who have been
forced to carry out their arduous duties at
the same time as child-rearing, because they
were the sole, or the partial, bread-winners.

The success of the women in munitions and
on land service lies partly in the fact that

they are uplifted with the thought that they are working for their country, that they are in fact needed; secondly, their way of living is healthy and regular, and they are nourished with good food at stated times; and thirdly, where women are employed in State-directed labour, there are supervisors and Welfare Workers whose main duty is to look after the health of the women, and see that they are doing work proportionate to their strength.

Rest-rooms are provided, and a trained nurse. The factory is one of the best in its organisation for women. It was started for women, and it was easier to begin on the right lines for dealing with women; whereas in the older factories great praise is due to the heads of the Arsenal that so much has been done for the women who have taken the place of the men.

Many of my own girls are here. The worthy man is also installed here, where he received promotion, and has rapidly won his way to popularity amongst the workers and staff. There are many links that bind us. The special health rules for the workers; a certain amount of risk in both factories; the means taken to prevent contact cases; the providing of milk, and the equipment of

workers, require from the Principal Overlookers
of both factories a series of responsibilities over
and above the general supervision and organisation of the women.

We did not say good-bye, but promised to
come again soon, for it was impossible to see
half of the working of this vast place in one
visit.   So we are still hoping at no very distant
time to return.

On our way back we pay a visit to the
Tailor's Shop.   The Tailor's Shop provides all
gowns, shoes, and caps; the blue serge fireproof coats and hats of Principal Overlookers;
the overlooker's badge or armlet, besides all
the men's clothing.

The overlooker's blue armlet is of special
interest to us, because we had petitioned for
a distinctive armlet.   The proposal was considered, and we further suggested that the
armlet should be of the blue serge like the
Principal Overlooker's coat, to show a logical
gradation between overlooker and P.O.   The
question was raised as to the need for every
factory in the Danger Buildings to have
the same badge for the overlooker.   At
length the proposal was carried, and on the
very day of our leaving the blue armlets
arrived, and were eagerly put on by the men

and women overlookers. The blue armlet is
easily seen on the cream gown or coat, and at
once shows the official who visits the factory
whom to address as overlooker.

The Tailor's Shop is an immense building.
Streets of tables with very narrow gangways
between are filled with women—machinists,
tailoresses, sempstresses, cutters-out—all the
large and varied gangs necessary to make,
mend, and enlarge all the Arsenal clothing for
men and women, and mark the covers and bags
for the various processes in the factories where
woven material of some sort comes into the
operation. Every worker in the Tailor's Shop
wears the mark of haste. Unlike the Danger
Buildings, where every operation must be careful and sure, the workers are possessed with
one aim, to turn out as much as possible in
the least possible time. The sewing machines
gallop, the scissors of the cutters-out fly along
the material, the very atmosphere is laden with
haste, and on every face we read that time
flies and we must hurry. The very idea of the
numbers they must clothe is stupendous ; the
practical execution of the demand is amazing.

The Paper Shop is similar in size, and in
the haste with which they perform their work.
Cardboard cases for fuses, and cardboard boxes

of various sizes for packing explosives—whatever is wanted in the way of paper or cardboard in the Arsenal, either in the actual operation or for packing—is carried out here.

Besides the garments and the paper, the shoe factory for the Arsenal shoe has its place here. The shoe department is part of the Tailor's Shop. It turns out hundreds of thousands for all the men and women whatsoever who work in Danger Buildings, as well as the overshoes that any chance official who enters wears, to go along the platforms and visit the workshops.

In concluding this brief and inadequate glimpse of women's factories, one may mention the number of women of standing who have hidden their identity and thrown in their lot with the great army of women workers. They are to be found amongst the workers and overlookers, as well as on the staff of the different factories. These women are doing very valuable work beyond their actual duties at their machines by setting up certain standards of living, by example and by sympathy. The ordinary worker does not wish to be obviously taught, far less preached to, but, being a reasonable being, and endowed with quick observation and critical powers, she sums up her neighbour by her actions,

and will note when these actions are unob-
trusive yet kind and generous.

The woman who first shows sympathy,
and has aims differing from the ordinary
worker, may be classed as a fool and be
watched with suspicion for a short while.
When time passes, and no self-interested
motive appears ; when a kind action rather
lessens the giver's chances of comfort, and no
obvious benefit accrues to her but the satisfaction and happiness of helping a fellow-
being, then full confidence is established, and
the workers give her their whole-hearted
affection and respect. And those workers
who are not hasty in giving their confidence
are the more staunch, the more true when
once it is given. A typical example comes
to my mind, but in any part of the Arsenal
it may be found.

One who is a sculptor by profession has
shut up her beautiful house in the west of
England, where artists and sculptors went
to dream and to plan out the masterpiece
of their lives in the happier days of peace.
She went through a course of machinery,
and passed successfully. She was appointed
as overlooker, and for some months worked
through the long hours of day or night shift,

encouraging and looking after her girls, and inciting them to enthusiasm by her own spiritedness and kindness.

I can see her now, coming home in the evening after a day bristling with small difficulties which she had triumphantly conquered, whether it were troublesome machines, which must be correctly adjusted to a special gauge, or new contract work which must be put through at a given time; or perhaps it is a question of gaining for her workers an extra few minutes beyond the hour at midday, to allow of their going to and returning from a new canteen which has been opened, and which takes some time out of their rest to reach. Though fatigue is too plainly visible, the spirit is wholly undaunted, and one sees the steadfast gleam in her eye, and the humorous smile breaking out as she chats of the day's episodes before settling down to write to her son at the front.

And her girls have learnt the meaning of that steadfast look, and will work their hardest to exceed their tally and earn her "well done"; and they have experienced the sympathy and kindness and womanliness of that undaunted spirit, and devotedly love and respect her.

CHAPTER IX

CANTEENS [1]

" I have been so great a Lover: filled my days
So proudly with the splendour of Love's praise.

  . . . . . .

These have I loved :
  White plates and cups clean gleaming ;
Wet roof beneath the lamp-light, the strong crust
Of friendly bread ; and many-tasting foods."
RUPERT BROOKE.

TO-DAY, if any visitor who has no work to perform in the Arsenal is allowed a peep into its activities, he would say, perchance, of the canteens, " Here is God's plenty."

Large canteens are in proximity to the factories, and as fast as one is finished, the increased numbers of women demand yet another. Satisfactory work can only be accomplished if the body is properly nourished ; and the canteens are a striking monument of the thought and labour which has been expended to equip the human machine with sufficient potential energy to carry through the

---

[1] See views of Canteens facing pp. 118–119.

long hours of work required in the speeding up of munitions.

When women were first admitted to munition factories, I was asked on my return from Red Cross work in France to undertake the supervision of women workers in a private factory. Special stress was laid on the necessity for proper nourishment and the arrangements made for the satisfactory working of meal hours. All went well during the day work; but at the end of a few days, having learnt several machines, we were asked to take the night-shift. For a week we worked, all being amateurs except one electrician, and we got out the tally. But after a few days every woman was feeling exhausted, because no arrangements had been made for meals during the night. The management merely presented each worker with a cup of tea and a halfpenny bun after five or six hours' work, and there were no means whatever of providing anything further until the breakfast at the usual time in the morning. The strain told upon all of us, and I was obliged to come up to town to see a specialist on account of eye trouble. This prevented me from continuing the work. But the need of solid meals at night for night workers was made a necessity,

8

and after one or two initial difficulties the food question has been successfully grappled with wherever there are munition factories.

In the Arsenal the canteen adminstration is under the Welfare Committees and the Y.M.C.A. Our Lady Superintendent receives any complaints made at the Welfare canteens, and pays the girls a friendly visit at times, while Lady Henry Grosvenor presides over the Y.M.C.A. canteens. Welfare Visitors are constantly in attendance at all canteens during the meal times, testing the quality and quantity of food, inquiring into any complaints that the workers make, and using their time partly in getting into touch with them. They give information to our girls about the Recreation Clubs, and distribute bills of concerts and meetings in connection with the Arsenal workers. The dinner-hour in the canteen is the great opportunity for meeting the workers, and arranging schemes for their general welfare or recreation.

Every canteen has a system of tickets from the value of $\frac{1}{2}$d. to 8d. Books of tickets may be bought for 2s. 6d. or 5s. No money is handed over the counter or paid for anything bought in the canteen, but tickets are given up to the attendants to the value of the food that is bought.

In the recently built canteens, for example, the ticket offices are circular erections placed at intervals down the middle of the canteen; the solid meals are served at one end from windows in front of the kitchen, which is partitioned off from the canteen. Here the women present an eightpenny ticket and receive a dinner of meat and vegetables. At another set of windows on the same side puddings are dispensed in return for a two-penny ticket. At the other end of the canteen tea, coffee, milk, fruit, biscuits, and cakes are served at an open buffet. This arrangement relieves congestion, separating the crowds who want their dinner into different parts of the building, and is a great improvement on the old plan of having the ticket windows and all the dispensing of the food on one side of the canteen.

Every canteen has a portion partitioned off for the overlookers' room. In a recently built canteen which supplies meals to a very large factory with a correspondingly large number of Principal Overlookers and forewomen, the space partitioned off is for Principal Overlookers only; but there are several canteens for light refreshments in this factory, and overlookers are provided for in another canteen.

It is essential that canteens should be bright,

airy, and scrupulously clean. An army of scrubbers are employed for floors, forms, and tables, which are scrubbed daily and nightly, looking spotless immediately after the scrubbing; but they become woefully dirty as soon as many thousands of feet have passed through for the midday meal, and have left again at the call to the workshops.

The canteens are lit by many windows, and those recently built have extra lights in the roof; they are painted white and green inside, so that they have a very fresh and airy appearance. As the workers steadily increase, so the canteens become more crowded, until the pressure is removed by opening a new one for the surplus. Thus we are ever increasing, ever advancing.

Recently a new canteen has been opened, which includes accommodation for our factory, and the majority of our workers now patronise the New Canteen, which is excellent in every respect.

The Old Canteen has always been a favourite. The food was always well cooked, and served thoroughly hot and in an inviting fashion. Presided over by Mr M——, the whole canteen staff — manager, manageress, chef, and attendants—all did their work with an air of unity and good fellowship. Nothing was a trouble. The chef used to make us special cakes and pastry for the breakfasts we sometimes gave to the several workshops when on night duty. We chose the night because it was the only time when a little extra work and seating-room could be arranged from the ordinary curriculum. Every moment is precious, every seat occupied, every attendant busy during the day-shift, making the giving of parties impossible.

The manageress added to an excellent gift of organising, ready tact and good-heartedness. One day, to quote an instance of general kindliness, there were no cups to be had in the overlookers' room when I ordered tea, except those supplied to the workers, of an amazing thickness. So she sent me a special cup presented to her by her staff, which was a valuable and beautiful thing, so that I should have my tea out of a nice cup. The act and kind heart which prompted it made the meal a feast, and turned weariness to joy. When I was specially tired, the cup would appear. I am still looking for a plate after the same pattern as that cup to present as a memento of that pleasant experience; but in order to present it, I must journey down to the New Canteen, where the trotyl workers are fed, for there the staff has been recently installed, and a Welfare staff has replaced them at the —— Factory. We had a pleasant surprise on the day we visited the trotyl factory. Our guides took us to lunch at the New Canteen, where I was led to expect that the management was excellent. There was a special dish of chicken and rice that day, served as we used to have it in the Cartridge Canteen. I remarked on this, and suddenly discovered that our old staff was established here ; a moment after the manager came forward with a smile of welcome and asked if I had come down here also. No, I replied, I was taking a holiday, but should like to come and work at this factory ultimately.[1]

Meat and vegetables can be bought for eightpence. At some of the Welfare canteens the price was sevenpence, and still remains so in spite of the general rise of all food. The Lady Superintendent tells me that they are paying their way as well. This is the highest tribute that can be paid to canteen management in the Arsenal. The meat course sometimes

[1] See a group of this Canteen, with Lady Henry Grosvenor, facing p. 118.

includes poultry: there is always a choice. Steak pudding or pie is one of the favourite dishes, but roast pork is *facile princeps.* The canteen staff has an uncomfortable time with late comers, so great is the annoyance when pork is on the menu and it has all disappeared by the time the stragglers enter. Still worse is it when those who have waited in the queue for their turn find that pork is off when they are at length served.

The —— Canteen devised a solution of this difficulty by placing on the bill of fare two favourite dishes together, or two ordinary ones. So that when one dish gave out, the other favourite was still to be had, and grumbling was reduced to a minimum. It might be a good plan for all canteens to work on this principle: it prevents undue disappointment among the workers.

Many a time some of my workers have accosted me on the platform, saying triumphantly, "Oh, miss! we had a *lovely* dinner to-day: roast pork *and* apple sauce : it was good." Hardly had I time to sympathise and congratulate them before more women arrived, looking dejected, even angry, and breaking forth, " Miss, it's a shime! *all* the roast pork was finished, and we were obliged to have

mutton." One terrible day they approached
me in the canteen, saying they could get nothing but bread and cheese. On inquiring we
found that an extra factory had sent down about
one hundred workers, and the extra numbers
had caused a meat shortage for the moment.
During the six months, I only heard of one
such occasion. Difficulties are quickly solved,
and inequalities balanced.

Besides the Canteen Committee, there are
the Welfare Visitors, who see that the workers
have no cause to grumble, and carefully sift
complaints which have no real foundation; for
the workers at times are both captious and
capricious; they are, however, proportionately
grateful when arrangements are to their satisfaction. There is also a representative committee elected from the munition workers by
the several factories using any given canteen.
The workers hand in suggestions and complaints to these representatives, and meetings
are held at stated intervals. It will therefore
be seen that every effort is made from within
and from without to give the best that is
possible for the munition workers in regard
to the canteen management.

Besides the paid staff a number of voluntary
workers are attached to the majority of the

A Canteen, Danger Buildings.

A Canteen, Non-danger Buildings.

[*To face p.* 118.

Workers as Girl Guides.

The Pageant: Joan of Arc and Warriors.

:el Group

The Pageant : French Peasants.

The Pageant : Joan of Arc and Knights.

A Group of Workers, X Factory.

A New Canteen, Danger Buildings.

canteens, who give either partial or whole time. As a rule they give their services at meal times, when there is great pressure, and devote their time to serving.

A piano is to be found in nearly every canteen, and affords a means of recreation that adds the last touch of happiness to the rest time, providing for amusement in the shape of singing and dancing. There was in my time one little canteen known to the Arsenal as the model. It was always clean, always cosy, and always managed to pay its expenses. Close to the X Shop, it provided for the workers from that busy hive, and also fed the Y Factory. The canteen is divided into two parts—the clean side, communicating with the factory, and the dirty side, which opens on to the roadway and admits the shop workers in their outdoor garments. The secret of the excellent management could be traced to two causes. First and foremost, the three friends who ran it lived for the canteen alone; all their thought and all their energy was expended on it, and their enthusiasm incited every attendant on the staff to look upon it as a sailor does his ship—a thing to be kept burnished and scrubbed and exquisitely clean. Secondly, meals were served at separate hours on the clean and on the dirty side, so that all the energies of the whole staff were devoted to one side or the other, and thus they met the difficulty of coping with enormous numbers.

Enter the canteen at the dinner time. The seats are filled by figures clad in creamy gowns, all looking supremely contented; for were they not in their own clean, "model" canteen, with kind waitresses to serve them, and food most invitingly cooked?

Facing the door is the buffet: behind the counter are the tables for the dinner course to be cut up and served, and further back, alongside the wall, are the arrangements for cooking in bulk: huge steamers for puddings and vegetables, cauldrons for making soup, and a series of cooking and heating ovens. The counter is invitingly laid out with piles of apples and oranges, pyramids of cakes; and at intervals are the brightly burnished urns; and serving here are the three ladies who manage the canteen with their voluntary staff, who are clad in heliotrope overalls and dainty little black silk caps. The pantry and store branches off from the kitchen. Everything is in its place, and the books are kept from hour to hour. Everything taken out is carefully recorded, and the book is balanced before the canteen is closed. In the store room, standing against a background of oranges and apples, biscuit tins and flour barrels, I saw the cook a little later in the afternoon, counting out kippers for the teas and piling them on to a snowy wooden platter. She herself was clad in butcher blue, with a white lace frilled cap, and I exclaimed to my friend, " I should like to sketch this interior." But the cook, with merry blue eyes aglow, said : " Oh, if you *do* take me, I must hold something important : let it be a sirloin of beef or a turkey, as it is the Christmas season." " No, no," I replied ; " nothing in the way of important joints could make up for the bright silvery hues of the scales contrasted with the red of the kipper on that snowy board, carried with such grace by the picturesque figure with the sunny countenance." At this reply she fled, and the next moment was busily engaged in getting us the cosiest and daintiest little tea I ever had in the Arsenal.

Besides the canteens which supply dinners and teas for the workers, there are many " short meal " establishments, where tea and coffee and anything in the way of light refreshments or tinned goods can be bought. At these places

the workers bring their own food, making
up with fruit, cakes, and light refreshments.
Such canteens have boilers and ovens where
workers can make their own tea and heat
their own meals. At different parts of the
Arsenal there are coffee stalls outside the
factory, but these are for the men.

The canteen management in the Arsenal
deserves high praise. The problem of feeding these vast numbers has been solved in
such a way as to allow good food at nominal
prices to be served in pleasant and, generally,
airy surroundings, thanks to the many men
and women who have brought their experience to bear on the matter, and to the many
hundreds of voluntary workers who have
gladly given their services to feed the women
who feed the machines, and thus feed the
army at the front with munitions. The voluntary workers have performed a noble work,
for it is not work that brings immediate thanks
or reward ; it is thoroughly hard, and often
seemingly unappreciated, but the workers
become devotedly attached to those ladies
who look after them, as well as all the attendants who supply their needs.

The workers at times are not easy to please.
They come in tired and exhausted, and the

least thing sometimes draws forth ill temper, whether there are grounds for complaint or not. At one canteen there was one day a choice between mutton and liver and bacon. All wanted liver and bacon, and the remainder grumbled at receiving mutton when all the liver and bacon was served. A few days after the same choice was on the bill of fare. A plentiful supply of liver and bacon was prepared. All chose mutton, and the remainder grumbled at the liver and bacon. An inquiry led to the statement that the liver and bacon a few days previously was not nice. Now the L.S. happened to be there on that particular day, and tested the liver and bacon, finding no just ground for complaint. So there is a certain margin of capriciousness to be allowed for. This is one of the difficulties in every canteen; but difficulties here or elsewhere are made to be solved. The best solution is that already given: to provide on certain days dishes which are equal favourites, and on other days dishes which are moderately liked.

The workers may ask for special dishes, if they bring an order from the doctor to that effect. Some require fish, others certain dishes which are provided if they are genuinely needed, on receipt of a doctor's certificate. At one canteen a worker asked for chop and chips ; it was not on the menu, and therefore not forthcoming. On stating that it was doctor's order, she was told that an order from the doctor would receive attention. A day or two after she produced the order for chop and chips, and for months she has received this dish day after day with complete satisfaction. In every canteen fish is served at least once a week for dinner, and kippers or bloaters are to be had for tea, when fish is procurable. The fish dinners at our canteen were always very good and very much liked.

After the meal there are deck chairs to be had at most canteens, where the workers rest and sleep, while others cluster round the piano and sing, and the remnant clear a space near by and dance. Paper and envelopes are procurable at the Y.M.C.A. canteens, and many workers employ their time during dinner or tea to write their letters to husbands or other relatives at the front.

The canteen is thus the centre of the life of the workers during the brief periods of rest. There are a few who like to retire to the Shifting-house, but it depends upon their affection for the special Shifting-house, and for the attendants who look after it. They are encouraged to use the canteens, which are so bright and cheerful; and so much is done for them that they do not require much persuasion.

The canteens have been the scenes of a more stirring, more anxious occasion. We remember one special night, when all our workers and those of a neighbouring factory had assembled for dinner. The majority had received their dinners, some were still waiting, when all lights were switched off, and there was utter darkness. To the discomfort was added the annoyance of losing dinners, for in the darkness some were lost, others were dropped and smashed. For a short space confusion reigned, but no one attempted to move, for it was safe to be in the dark, safe to be in the canteen; they all had seats, and could at least rest. Calm was soon restored by groping to the piano, and finding somebody to play. A popular song was started, and soon about two thousand voices were singing. One song after another was sung, until at length, as the hours crept on, excitement and weariness induced sleep, and more than half leaned their arms on the tables, or slipped on to the floor underneath the tables. We were very proud of our girls that night. We walked up and down the gangway chatting, and cheering them, now comforting a mother who was anxious for her children at home, now clasping a hand stretched out in the darkness. And once before dawn, some fruit was thrust into my hand, and a whispered voice said, " It's good fruit, miss : you've had no dinner."

They are fearful before the coming of an air-ship or Zeppelin, but when it is in the neighbourhood they are perfectly calm and quiet, though some wish to sing, and others like to be perfectly still. All enjoy the singing, however, and it is the very best way to keep them occupied, as it has been found in all factories, I believe.

It was almost worth while to have the responsibility, on this particular night, to realise how bravely our lasses could hold themselves ; and when their voices rang out in the singing, we felt at one with our gallant sailor-lads who sang as the water closed over them ; at one with our soldiers in the trenches who sang in the fury of an attack, or an advance. Here there was unity from end to end of the Empire. And so we waited, while the cannonading could be heard all round us, and in the midst of us. Right across the sky was the gilded Thing which shot across our vision, riding high in the heavens; a moment after a smoke bomb hid it in volumes of cloud, and it vanished in an easterly direction. But the cannonading continued fierce, incisive, incessant; another hung in the sky, found and held by our search-lights. We hardly dared breathe as shell after shell from all sides rose to a hair's-breadth of that death-carrier. Suddenly it pitched head foremost, turned, and was straightened again, then dived over and seemed to burst from the centre into a great crimson red flare shot with gold and jagged blackness all round; then down, down, increasing in size and in the multiplicity of flaming light until the whole heavens seemed ablaze. A moment of intense silence that seemed eternity, then from myriads of unseen voices wave upon wave of cheering. We realised then that this was not an episode of the Arsenal, but all the millions in and around London had looked on breathless at the struggle, and their pent-up feelings were now having vent.

So it fell, as Satan fell when there was war in heaven and Michael and his angels conquered; it fell as morning was breaking over the earth, and shafts of light were dispersing the darkness. And the stars of the morning sang together,

9

and never had the earth seemed more lovely, never had the heavens enfolded us with such security, never had the Everlasting Arms seemed so near, as darkness and the terror, and the nearness of death passed away, and in one's heart and brain rang the notes of the glorious chorus, " Watchmen, what of the night ? The night is departing, the day is at hand." And all creation seemed to pulse with the exulting notes of the concluding hymn of praise, " The day is at hand."

Then we turned to normal things, and superintended the distribution of boiling tea and cocoa to the famished and cold women and girls. Half an hour later, at 5 a.m., we paid our usual rounds to the workshops. All operations were in hand, and the only difference to be detected from the normal was the tense expression on the faces of the elder women, and the whole-hearted energy in the work of the younger ones. And one spoke the mind of the whole factory when she said to me, " We must work our very hardest to make an end of those Zeps."

CHAPTER X

" Con pace ogn' opra sempr' al fin assalto."
MICHAEL ANGELO.

(" All things have rest upon their journey's end.")
Trans. by J. ADDINGTON SYMONDS.

THE housing of the women is no less important than the feeding of them, and to a
certain extent the organisations coalesce.
Many hostels have the catering part managed
by the Y.M.C.A. Committee. This arrangement is a saving in many ways. The same
method is observed in dealing with supplies ;
and those who have the provisioning of the
canteens can best judge numbers and quanti-
ties, and also know what the tastes of the
workers are.

Apart from the catering, a good deal of wise
management is required in looking after the
workers during their hours of rest and recreation. One large hostel called the " Joan of

Arc " is capable of housing 700 munition
workers. The Eltham Hostel is built to provide
for 2500. Round and near Woolwich Common
are Y.W.C.A. houses, and boarding-houses
adapted for workers. To-day there is no
difficulty in finding rooms, as the early workers
experienced ; but a little over a year ago
rooms were scarce and proportionately dear,
and there were one or two regrettable ex-
periences, where a lodger found, being on the
night-shift, that her room was let to someone
else when she was not in possession. But the
hostels were built in a surprisingly short time,
and the care of hostels includes some of the
most cherished schemes for the health, comfort,
and happiness of working women. The Queen
Mary Hostel was opened in the autumn to
accommodate many of the ladies who came
from various parts of the British Isles, as well
as our Colonies, to help in the management
as superintendents of canteens, principal overlookers, and overlookers, or as voluntary
canteen workers.

The hostels are built on the principle of the
large military hospitals. The whole building
is a settlement of bungalows connected by
streets of corridors. On either side of the
corridor are the workers' rooms. The middle

of the block is occupied by a dining hall connected with kitchen and its accessory offices. The dining hall connects with another room running the entire length. In the case of the Queen Mary Hostel, this room is fitted up as a lounge, with plenty of really comfortable chairs and sofas. Windows are on three sides, fireplaces at intervals on either side of the room. There is artistic colouring, and the mode of decoration is similar to an old manorial hall, the arched roof composed of oak beams; electric lights are suspended from them by chains, and silken shades of warm tones add a charming touch of colour. These were the gift of a friend, and were much appreciated. All through the winter lovely flowers were sent us. Clusters of show chrysanthemums, winter roses, and masses of Michaelmas daisies cheered the weary guests when they arrived after their day or night's labour. Lady Henry Grosvenor is now in residence here, and personally supervises the arrangements for the comfort of all. We had the good fortune to meet with kindred spirits on our arrival last September. A lady, well known for her social charm, as well as her intrinsic merit, welcomed us and looked after our comfort with the geniality of a hospitable hostess and the sym-

pathy and thought of a mother.   We founded
an Arts table.   It included a niece of Thomas
Carlyle, an artist, a sculptor, a writer or two,
a niece of Lord Morley's, and later, a relative
of Sir Oliver Lodge.   Many of the original
members dispersed for other duties as time
passed on, but the Arts table is still kept
sacred, and when any original member returns,
we always move to that special table.   One
charming Belgian lady is with us, doing
munitions while her relatives are fighting on
the Somme front.   The great hour of the day
is tea-time, when sundry groups gather round
the various fires and make toast, feeling as if
college days had returned.

The inmates of the " Joan of Arc " are mostly
young working girls.   They have an abund-
ance of spirits and like plenty of amusement.
The directress has done much for them in the
way of very able administration and sympathetic insight into the character and needs
of the girls.

Twice a week recreation takes the form of
a dance, when the workers may invite a friend
in khaki.   Invitations are by card only, and
are sent out from the office.   Both guest and
worker are responsible for the mutual good
behaviour, and they have responded to the

trust reposed in them ; for the dances, initiated as a social experiment, are a complete success. The band of the garrison is lent on these occasions, and "official" visitors, including the L.S., Welfare Visitors, and others of the staff often join in the amusement of the evening.

This hostel was the first to have a chapel, which was established through the personal endeavours of Miss M——, the directress. Time has proved what a boon this is to many of her workers. Simply and tastefully furnished in tones of blue, the chapel is open at an early hour in the morning. On Sundays, too, when the khaki "boys" come to tea with our girls, they often join in the simple service afterwards. The need has been felt elsewhere, and chapels are being placed in other hostels. The Archbishop of Canterbury has also recently arranged for a chapel to be added to the Queen Mary Hostel. It is now being built.

Above the Joan of Arc Hostel flies the flag with their Patroness heroine emblazoned thereon, copied from the original at Rouen. On p. 118A a group of girls is shown standing round their flag, with Miss M—— and Miss P—— in the foreground. The group is of especial interest, for the girls are wearing

their uniform of Girl Guides, recently insti-
tuted in this hostel. Thus the spirit of service
and patriotism inherent in the name Joan of
Arc permeates the whole building.

A fine opportunity came at the time of the
fête in July for the workers to show their
zeal. A pageant of Joan of Arc was arranged
and carried through with great success (see
p. 118A). The heroine, who is a P.O. and has
been an inmate of the Joan of Arc Hostel since
its opening, had the time of her life in learning
to ride a splendid horse lent by the garrison,
and riding it, in the guise of the illustrious
girl-warrior, on the day of the pageant.

The arrangements are slightly different at
the Eltham Hostel. Workers need dinner and
tea at the Arsenal, and many like to come home
and have a light meal before going to rest.
The Eltham Hostel does not cater for dinners,
but provides food as it is wanted ; and many
girls prefer this way of living, for they pay for
their room, and buy on the spot any food they
require. In the other hostels breakfast and
dinner is provided, and the Sunday's meals.
Since a good, wholesome dinner is provided
in the Arsenal, and tea or breakfast, which
can be made into a high tea according to the
needs of the workers, this arrangement of the

Eltham Hostel seems a satisfactory one, and is of course less expensive for the worker who is not receiving high wages.

The Eltham Hostel occupies a large area. It is now divided into two sections. The near side continues to be used as the residential quarters for women munition workers; the far side is now open for men workers.

Each side has its administrative block and residential quarters for its staff of women and men respectively. The whole organisation is directly under the head of the Welfare Committee in the Arsenal, whereas the other hostels are under Y.M.C.A. management.

A group of the Eltham Hostel is inserted on p. 118A, showing in the foreground the principal members of the Welfare Committee, including the Superintendent of the Arsenal, the L.S., and various officers of the Eltham Hostel staff.

As usual, the hostel contains streets of bungalows, with the workers' rooms on either side of the corridors. It differs, however, in possessing a sitting-room and writing-room on every corridor. This is a recent addition and is much appreciated.

There is a general recreation room, and a large canteen instead of a dining-room. The canteen possesses a stage, and half the canteen can be curtained off when necessary to form an auditorium when entertainments are held.

A chapel was opened here in July. The Government provided building and seating. Each corridor contributed to the furnishing, and much labour and ingenuity was shown in the contribution of kneelers, and cushions for the chancel-rail, all done by hand. The altar furnishing was also contributed, and the dossal and lectern hangings made by a member of the staff. The latest addition is a new harmonium, the combined gift of the hostel.

The Welfare Workers are in touch with all the hostels. They visit individual girls when occasion arises through absence, or some other cause. They also visit the hostels when any special concert or dance is given, and join in the festivity. Besides the individual hostel recreations, there is the Women's Recreation Club, specially founded for those living in the hostels; for the hostel inmates are near at hand, whereas those who live in their own homes are often too far away to take part in any amusement after the hours of work. All kinds of classes are arranged to suit the wishes of the workers. The girls learn gymnastics, dancing, singing, elocution: they have asked for First-Aid classes, dressmaking, and embroidery. The L.S. is willing to arrange any class when it is asked for by some eight or ten members, and she always finds a keen and willing exponent to run the special class when formed. The club hours are arranged between the shifts, so that night workers can attend for an hour before going to work, day workers can enter before returning home. In connection with the club, occasional concerts are arranged, and weekly Sunday concerts were started in the New Year. There is latterly an endeavour to form a choral society, but the difficulty of getting the required voices together at the same time is somewhat of a difficulty, as the hours of recreation are so short. As the weeks pass there is always some new scheme being added for the benefit of the worker when she has finished work, just as inside the factory there is continual advance for the health and general well-being of the workers.

The year 1917 has seen steady progress in every part of Arsenal life without and within, the two special outside features being the great Fête in July, with the Joan of Arc Pageant, and the Mission in September. Inaugurated by the Archbishop of Canterbury, four hundred Missioners, including several

Bishops, have carried out a Crusade; and Beresford Square has been the unwonted scene of a gathering for prayer and sacred song for the crowds that habitually gather there.

The Welfare Workers are the people who weld the work-a-day life with the home life, getting into touch with the workers, and learning to know them in shop, in canteen, in the hostel, and even in the home. So we are preparing for the future, that when the war ends our women and girls will be the healthier and the happier, and more able to make cleaner and brighter and purer homes for their men folk when they return.

CHAPTER XI

THE PAY OFFICE

" For the labourer is worthy of his hire."
St Luke's Gospel.

ARSENAL life is not fully known until the weekly concourse has been observed in the large spaces at the back and front of the pay office, where the factories are paid in groups.

The handing over of the pay to each worker once a week is the last act of a series of processes involving many hundreds of clerks, who are busied day and night with checking attendance lists, totalling the number of hours worked, marking changes in rates and shares, according to the occupation. The shifting of a worker from one shop to another often involves a difference in pay.

Work-takers are appointed to every factory, who visit each workshop during the morning and the afternoon, checking the attendance lists, noting absentees, and inserting the occupation of every worker. Every shifting from one occupation to another must be recorded, in order to obtain the correct time-sheet, and the pay resulting. The D.P.O. must know the rates and shares of every occupation, and see that every worker is paid accordingly. The D.P.O. must advise the office of any change, increase, or decrease arising thereby, and any question must go through her to the pay office representative, who visits the factory once or twice a week.

The pay office, then, has a complex task in exploring the ramifications of the pay-sheets. Besides the weekly pay, there is the sick and injury pay; and the weekly pay includes such adjustments as extra time, Sunday time, night-rate work, war bonus, the subtraction of hours for lateness and for absence. The picking up of the ticket in the morning denotes presence and punctual attendance: the late comer finds the ticket office closed. The attendance is marked at the assembling in the workshops by the D.P.O., and her list is sent up. Any discrepancy between the D.P.O.'s list and the people who fail to pick up their tickets is noted. The work-takers go their rounds and mark attendance. So it is quite impossible for any absentee to escape notice. The same routine is gone through after the dinner-hour. The D.P.O. sends up her absentee lists. The worker-takers go their rounds, mark attendance, and occupation of each worker. After tea, the D.P.O. makes her final round for absentees, and sends the list to the office. Those who leave at tea-time are obliged to hand their tickets over to the attendants. By this method the attendance and hours of work are exactly compiled.

The representative from the pay office makes his rounds during the week, and any difficulty is unravelled, any question answered involving rates of pay and value of shares. More than one half-hour was spent going through the intricacies of the time-sheet with him, when he explained the method of totalling up the week's payments and the various calculations required. I always left him thankful that my duties did not include the compilation of the weekly payments; but he carried his duties with a cheeriness that was never clouded by pressure of work, or dimmed by the various demands made upon his patience. He was one of the pleasantest of the number of kindly people it was our good fortune to meet amongst those who had come together to work for the period of the war in this great centre of labour.

Every Thursday afternoon one noted an air of pleasant anticipation throughout the workshops, intensified as the hour drew near for departure. The hootah went ten minutes earlier to give time to change and reach the pay office by 6.50. The women were divided between anxiety to get to the pay office and the desire to look their best, for on pay night they often went shopping, or met a friend and spent the evening at some place of amusement. The D.P.O. could not wait until the Shifting-house was empty on these occasions, because her duty was at the pay office, marshalling her women into lines before their respective doors in numerical order. The worker is paid by her ticket number and not her name, and she receives her ticket number on a card with the amount to be paid to her before she leaves the factory.

Arrived at the door, the scene is like the early doors at a favourite theatre, only one must imagine a large number of theatres close together, and innumerable queues waiting at the long line of doors and windows outside the pay office. The casual observer will see nothing but a confused sea of heads, and what appears to be a tumult; but inside the crowd it will be noticed that the knots and groups are disentangling themselves, and finding their right places in the queues that are being formed The D.P.O. walks down the lines receiving the number of each woman as she passes, and inspecting the tickets, which everyone must hold in her right hand in readiness to show and give up in return for the pay. It is necessary to carefully watch for the new entries and for late comers. The former lose their heads completely, and want to dive into any place that looks easy of access, and it requires a good deal of piloting and urging on the part of the D.P.O. to get her correctly placed. She is then told to notice who is in front of her, and to remember to keep the same place on future occasions. The late comers, anxious to be paid, will rush up to the door and try to squeeze through, in their desire to be paid without undue waiting. They also are put in a place apart, until the others have been paid, and they are then hurried through by the courtesy of the pay office officials, and by the importunity of the D.P.O., who has no desire to wait until the next factory is paid, before her erring late workers get their pay. Prompt passing

10

through always helps us; for if we have a minute to spare out of the ten minutes allowed for our factory, we pass our late arrivals through. If the time for payment is past, and the next factory is due, it would be necessary to wait. But during my six months' duties, we never had to wait for any defaulters of our factory, and very few women were late. For we always came through the pay office with a minute or half a minute at least to spare, which gave us time to clear off late workers. This satisfactory state of affairs was largely due to the help of our men colleagues.

The twenty minutes at the pay office is certainly one of the most exciting periods in the week. For ten minutes chaos is being reduced to order with every faculty and every atom of energy we possess. It must be done with lightning speed. The next ten minutes is spent in taking them through, and bundling the late ones through on the heels of our queue. With a cheerful sense of a task fulfilled we bid good night to the foreman and pass out. On pay day we are one of the first to leave the Arsenal, for we hurry to catch an early tram or train; whereas on this particular night of the week the women collect in front of the pay office and look at the amounts to

see that they are correct, and chat with their
friends before they saunter out of the Arsenal.
The younger and noisier ones generally sing
lustily ; the older women are quiet as a rule,
anxious to get to their homes and their children ;
but all look upon Thursday night as a break in
the routine of the week and a time of meeting
and relaxation—either for a few minutes, or
for the whole evening.   Pay day to the general
worker is a milestone of life.   Every Friday
begins a fresh period until the following
Thursday, which culminates at the time of
payment.

CHAPTER XII

"The morning will surely come, the darkness will vanish, and thy voice pour down in golden streams breaking through the skies." RABINDRANATH TAGORE.

OUR lasses began to talk of Christmas and to sing carols over their work as early as November. The burning question on the lips of all was whether there would be a holiday, and, if so, how many days.

This question was asked "ad infinitum," and was at first met by that most disheartening reply, "We must wait and see." But as the question was repeated day after day, we used to say : "It will certainly depend upon us all. If we are never late for the next few weeks, and take no time off whatever, and work our very hardest, we may be rewarded. For we must be quite certain that the country cannot afford to do without munitions for some days, unless between now and then we manage by absolute punctuality to put out the extra munitions, so that the holiday may not be detrimental to output." The few weeks preceding the New Year were certainly marked by very good attendance. The Welfare Workers demurred at my failing to send in a list of absentees for inquiry, and I replied that the attendance had been exceptionally good, and only two cases needed attention. There were, however, two disastrously foggy days which stopped traffic, and many who tried to walk got lost. An amusing story was told of a foreman who knew the factory thoroughly. He stumbled across one of our women who had lost her way in the Arsenal between the entrance gate and the factory. " Come along with me," said the foreman ; " I will put you right." An hour and a half later two forlorn people found themselves at a distant gateway of the Arsenal, more than a mile away from the factory, but by perseverance they at length reached the factory, and entered like heroes about nine o'clock in the evening.

Two volunteer workers also on that night left our factory about seven o'clock, and some hours later they entered again asking, " Is this the Arsenal gate ? " having wandered round and returned to the starting place without knowing it.

The good attendance was also partly due to
the fact that the workers wanted full over-
time pay. They had Christmas presents and
dinners to send to their dear ones at the
front ; they had parcels to send to their prisoner
relatives ; and they remembered that if they
were going to get a holiday, there would be
some days without pay.

At length the great news was posted up on
the Arsenal gates and in every Shifting-house.
Government had fixed a holiday for munition
workers from the 22nd to 27th of December.
How elated everyone was ! Our shift discovered with much glee that they, being on
day-shift, would be able to leave on Thursday
night, and would not return until the following Wednesday night for the night-shift. So
it seemed that they had nearly a week, and
great was the satisfaction. The weather
changed too. The week before Christmas Day
was bright and frosty, and we all enjoyed the
walk up the Straight on the frozen ground, our
senses quickening with the exhilaration of the
keen air.

The week was marked by a general giving and receiving of presents amongst the
workers. It was their first Christmas season
in the Arsenal ; it might be, as everyone

hoped, the last under war conditions. So they celebrated the event. And it marked their happiness and general well-being in the life spent in busy work and pleasant intercourse. All the workers knew that they were going to have their Christmas holiday in their own homes, but these few days served as their Christmas together in the Arsenal. They arranged tea-parties, and when the week had advanced to Wednesday, there was a feeling amongst them that Thursday, the day appointed for the holiday, must be specially kept and be made as festive as possible.

At dinner-time the canteen presented a very festive appearance: special decorations, and festive extras at the buffet in the shape of mince-pies and Christmas fruits.

The L.S. came down, and was in time to carve the turkey, which was supplied for a slightly extra charge. She then visited each table and spoke a word of seasonable greeting to the diners. Nobody dawdled over dinner, for they were bent on making merry. A crowd formed at the piano, and songs and dancing began. Before we were aware we were drawn into the festivity. The L.S. laughed merrily as she caught sight of us being whirled round by eager dancers, but a moment afterwards she, too, was caught and joined the merry throng. And we all enjoyed it, and the girls, realising that, were correspondingly happy.

The factory was divided throughout that afternoon by the desire to work well, the feeling of subdued excitement at the approaching holiday, and the immediate happiness of their last meal in the canteen at tea-time. Many were the little festive tea-parties arranged, with mince-pies for the special dish. Numerous invitations were pressed upon the D.P.O. to have tea with them; and to every invitation she replied that she would come down, though she inwardly wondered what quantity of mince-pie and what amount of dancing could be experienced for the happiness of her workers, without complete prostration upon the actual Christmas Day, on which occasion her small nephews and nieces regard her as their special property.

We gathered in the canteen, every lassie wearing a sprig of mistletoe, were it only a berry or a single leaf. Not a moment was wasted, and in a very short time tea and hot cakes and mince-pies were eaten, while the D.P.O. greeted the various tables, and had tea here and a mince-pie there. Everyone adjourned to the piano, and a small concert took place. In the midst of a very sad song, thoroughly enjoyed by the audience, the hootah went for return. The D.P.O. mentioned that it was time. Nobody stirred, and a request was made to have the last verse. It was the one festive night of the year to these lasses, so we sang the last verse, and the D.P.O. joined in. Then " God save the King " was sung. Three cheers were proposed for the lads and relatives at the front, and the canteen rang again to the response. Then they struck up a two-step and danced madly in long lines hand in hand. But their faces were towards the door, and in two minutes they were out and on their way to the workshops singing and crying, " Three cheers for the D.P.O."

A few minutes later we went the rounds, and they were all quietly at work, only their faces were radiantly happy, and at our entry they started clapping.

We wished them a Happy Christmas, saying, in the trite way, that it only came once a year. They understood that the especial privilege was for that night only, and they did not take advantage of it. They were just thoroughly happy, and had enjoyed to the full their little festivity together. The hootah sounded for leaving, and away they went. At the door of the Shifting-house we shook hands with all, wishing them a pleasant holiday. Auntie Ellis and Auntie May were gladdened by a literal Christmas box in which everyone dropped pennies, and this gave them a substantial Christmas present. The two water-carriers had a similar box, so all went away really happy, with the happiness that innocent enjoyment brings. We knew that every soldier and sailor would do his best to have a good time at this season, and in the quiet solemnity of that evening's walk to the gates it seemed as if Heaven had decreed an armistice for the whole world, for the coming of the Christ Child, that Peace might be once more upon the earth for a brief season.

Friday was spent in arranging the Christmas gifts contributed by the workers' Christmas donation to our Red Cross Fund. The table for St John's Relief Hospital was purchased, and two convalescent soldiers from St John's met it at the station and carried it delightedly up the hill. One soldier ate his Christmas dinner off it, and the others used it at the party in the evening.

Gifts were also sent to the Red Cross Hospital in Florence, which bought electrical apparatus for special treatment. Letters were received in the New Year from members of the Committee and from the Secretary expressing gratitude for the thought and gifts of the munition workers. And the next gift required is a chair for one of the French hospitals to be sent through the French Emergency Fund, in memory of the undying glory of the French at Verdun ; and we hope to make this our next Christmas gift. Meanwhile, more crutches have been sent to both English and French hospitals with the balance of the Fund.

Once more we gathered together in the Shifting-house on New Year's morning to hear the rules. The New Year had dawned brightly, and it was a world of sun and blue sky as the day advanced. A cheery crowd had assembled, and the D.P.O. climbed aloft as usual in order to face her audience. She wished them a Happy New Year, and hoped, when the year was old, the war would be over and every lassie in some good employment. Then the rules were recited, repeating and dwelling upon those most liable to be broken. Once more good wishes, a responsive cheer, and the crowd flowed out along the platforms to their respective shops.

A few days later they called me to the Shifting-house, and when I arrived, it was they who had climbed into posts of eminence to see and to talk to me. And the words of those lasses went straight down to my heart, and there they remain " too deep for words." And I have their precious gifts, and constantly use them. In fact, this book has been written with the pen, and the MS. has been carried in the beautiful little case for the last few months. And each one of their faces I remember, and shall not forget. We had come to the end of our six months together, and had learnt much from one another. In their own words, they " have got used to me,"[1] and, knowing that, it is with much regret that we say good-bye, and go on to the fresh work that calls. For we must all work, not for the end of the war only, but for the great settling and arranging of our land when peace shall have come. The end of war will be but the beginning of that period, and we shall all be needed to do whatever work is then most desired from us, whether it be in the home or work outside.

In that beautiful old Greek story of the

[1] To get used to, in Arsenal language, is a highly complimentary term.

wanderings of Ulysses after the Trojan war,
Penelope, the wife of Ulysses, cared for her
husband's estate, brought up their son, worked
and kept faith with the absent one through
long years of trial, while might tried to conquer
right, and she was beset without and within.
At length Ulysses returns in disguise and
realises with a great passion of love how
Penelope has worked and waited and loved.
And he throws off his disguise and breaks
the power of might, utterly conquering the
enemy.   And after that there is a great
cleansing of the house that it may be worthy
of Penelope, and they settle down in happy
contentment to manage their home and estate.

So with us: every home must be brighter
for the welcoming of father, husband, or
brother.   And if every home is more lovely,
then England, Britain, our Empire, will be
more happy and more true.

In that glad day the bells will ring out
once more over our Empire, and in temples
made with hands, as in all nature, one joyous
song of thanksgiving shall be sung to the
King of kings.   And Britain, the mother
country, joining hands with her sons and her
daughters across the seas, shall settle down
once more to her responsibilities and to the

managing of her great estates. And in the Houses of Westminster, with the flag floating free above them, the voices of the representatives from the over-sea Dominions shall mingle their voices with Britain's leaders, working together for the common weal of the Empire, and for the mutual prosperity of our brave Allies. So, for all who will work well, and love well, and keep faith well, " the morning will surely come, and the darkness will vanish, and the golden streams will pour down breaking through the skies."

Ingram Content Group UK Ltd.
Milton Keynes UK
UKHW020220250323
419164UK00009B/32